Ethical

Ethical

What You Must Know to Build Trust
and Maintain Genuine Relationships

Dr. Daniel Morris

Ethical – Dr. Daniel Morris
Copyright © 2015
First edition published 2015
All rights reserved. No part of this book may be reproduced, stored in a retrieval system, or transmitted in any form or by any means – electronic, mechanical, photocopying, recording, or otherwise, without written permission from the publisher.

Scripture quotations are taken from the Holy Bible, King James Version, Cambridge, 1769.

Cover Design: Amber Burger

Cover Photography: mamanamsai/Shutterstock

Editors: Sheila Wilkinson, Ruth Zetek

Printed in the United States of America
By Aneko Press – *Our Readers Matter*™
www.anekopress.com
Aneko Press, Life Sentence Publishing, and our logos are trademarks of
Life Sentence Publishing, Inc.
203 E. Birch Street
P.O. Box 652
Abbotsford, WI 54405

RELIGION / Christian Education / Adult
Paperback ISBN: 978-1-62245-253-8
Ebook ISBN: 978-1-62245-252-1

10 9 8 7 6 5 4 3 2 1
Available wherever books are sold.

Share this book on Facebook

Contents

Everyday Ethical Situations IX

Introduction XIII

Ch. 1: Four Fundamental Principles of Ethics 1

Ch. 2: Knowing When to Obey or Counter Authority 9

Ch. 3: Ethical Treatment of Things We Don't Own 23

Ch. 4: Ethical Handling of Finances 41

Ch. 5: Hospitality – Why Our "Best" is Not Always Right .. 61

Ch. 6: Ethical Agreements 65

Ch. 7: Proper Behavior Between the Opposite Sex 69

About the Author 75

I would like to give special thanks to my sister Doyla who is serving as a missionary to Australia along with her husband, Bill. She is not only a wonderful example for other Christians, but she also spent many hours helping with the editing of this book.

Everyday Ethical Situations

Example #1

The phone rang and Pastor John Green answered. On the other end of the line, George Carney, the pastor of a new, fast-growing church, greeted him. He explained that he had spoken with Mary, a secretary in John's church, about the great need that existed in his own church for a secretary. George had met Mary at a conference, and she had made a good impression on him. He had asked if she would consider working in a new church that had a need for help, and had already told her about the position's above-average pay and perks. Mary had expressed enthusiasm about the job he was offering.

George asked John if he would agree to this and requested a recommendation for Mary. Many thoughts went through John's mind. He found himself faced with a dilemma. Mary had grown up in his church and was a member. He had a close friendship with her and her family. However, she had many immature attitudes and character problems that he, as pastor, was trying to correct.

Because of this, if John gave a good recommendation, he could cause a problem for his friend George. On the other hand, if he gave an honest, negative recommendation, Mary would probably know why she lost the job offer. This could cause a conflict with her and perhaps her entire family.

Example #2

What pleasure it gave to Pastor Charles Doan to visit the city in which he had pastored a church for many years. Only two years had passed since he left to accept the pastorate in another church. He decided to visit one of the most cherished families of his former church, and he was received with joy.

After talking about their experiences and the well-being of their families, Charles asked how the church was doing. The family had seen much change with the new pastor and found it difficult to relate to him. Charles had been very open and dynamic, while the new pastor was more quiet and conservative. The new pastor also had some differences in priorities in the ministries. For this family, things were not the same as before.

With the confidence they felt in the presence of their former pastor, they began to express their feelings of doubt about their new pastor. This eventually led to criticizing him. Charles listened because this family was not happy. In some areas, he agreed with them. Although he didn't verbalize his thoughts, they could tell he empathized with them. Outwardly, he advised them to be patient and then redirected the conversation.

On Sunday, Steve Oliver, the new pastor, graciously welcomed this family but felt a intensified barrier between him and the family. Over time, this barrier developed into much contention, and he found he could not build up this family because they were not open to his counsel. He knew that the previous pastor maintained contact with them. This caused doubts about that former pastor's motives in visiting the church, and it even affected the relationship that both pastors had enjoyed before.

Example #3

A year had passed since Karla Jason had borrowed money from Alexander Barns, a member of Karla's church. Karla had promised to return the money in a month, but she spent the money on other items she thought were necessary. She admitted that sometimes she spent money not only on her needs, but also on things that were simply personal desires. Alexander was friendly and did not insist on repayment. She intended to pay him some day, but that day never seemed to come.

Alexander and Karla always greeted each other politely, but now the question was in his mind: *Will I ever be paid, or is she just going to keep my money?* He felt too embarrassed to ask her about the money and feared she would be annoyed if he mentioned it.

The sad thing was that a businessman friend was looking for someone to hire for a good job. Alexander could not recommend Karla even though she needed a job. He appreciated her as a friend, but he could not respect her word and had no confidence in her honesty. Therefore, he could not recommend her to the businessman and risk causing problems for his friend.

Example #4

The meeting was tense. The ten members of the corporate board of the Christian school had to make a decision. The school had ministered for many years in this city, but the campus maintenance was expensive. They had been offered a better school complex in another city. If they sold the current complex, they could buy the other campus and have money left over for improvements.

Many people, however, had labored and sacrificed to give money to buy the current campus. They would probably not understand the benefits of moving the school to another city. Some of the donors were leaders who could influence others to take a stand against the relocation. If the board announced their intentions in advance, they could be facing legal attempts to prevent the change.

These ten men acknowledged that many people had been responsible for the original purchase of the current complex, but they were also convinced that they knew what was best. After all, they had the legal right to sell the campus without the consent of the donors and felt it was their responsibility to make the decision. They believed the change would be the best decision, and others would eventually understand.

However, after the sale of the complex became known, many donors, parents of students, and students themselves were greatly divided. Some accepted the reasons for the change, but many felt disregarded and defrauded. Friendships from years back were broken, and conflicts abounded. Some people even threatened to sue.

****

In each of these four examples, private and public conflicts caused great damage to relationships and reputations. Alternatives existed that could have eliminated these conflicts and might have resulted in strengthening relations and respect. This book is a guide for understanding the harm of wrong ethical choices, finding a solution based on the principles of ethics, and solving problems without threatening relationships.

I had searched for a book on this subject to use in the discipleship program of the churches and missions in the state of Chiapas, Mexico. I could not find what I needed, and the thought occurred to me that perhaps I should write such a book. I resisted the idea because writing is neither fun nor easy for me, but rather is tiring and time-consuming.

However, God impressed upon me his love for his children and his desire for them to enjoy good relationships. The purpose was greater than the work and risk. I hope it will bring peace and stability to the lives of God's children and churches and, thereby, joy to God's own heart.

Introduction

Many times in life we must choose how to react to a situation or person. These decisions determine the quality of our experiences and affect our personal relationships. They also form the impression that others have of us – our reputation.

Many factors influence us to act one way rather than another. People do not all think alike, and this lends itself to disagreements and misunderstandings, which can cause resentment and conflict.

Who is right? The answer to this question depends on two concepts. The first is that if our decisions are made based on our personal opinions, likes and dislikes, or current feelings or convenience, then no one can say who is right. Why is one person right and another person wrong about tastes, feelings, or what is convenient? One person will not feel less intelligent than another in the decision-making process. As a result, harmony or agreement might not be possible among people with different opinions and preferences.

The other concept is that a universal agreement regarding what is good or bad behavior and what is right or wrong will be a foundation for understanding and harmony. With basic principles of how to determine right and wrong, we are more likely to know and choose the correct way to behave. The principles that determine correct behavior are called *ethics*.

Let's analyze the words *ethics* and *ethical*.

First, we are social beings who have ongoing relationships with each other.

Second, we affect each other through our practices, manners, and conduct.

Third, what we do can be good or bad, and this may affect the rights and well-being of others.

Fourth, because of the potential for problems and conflicts in these relationships, principles and regulations must determine what is right, what is respectful of others' rights, and what promotes the well-being of all.

Fifth, these principles and regulations cannot be opinions or matters of personal taste, but must be based on divine laws that God has established for humanity.

A philosophy of life based on the divine laws of God is called *ethics*. If we were writing a dictionary, we might define *ethics* as "the principles and regulations based on divine laws related to the practices, manners, and conduct of mankind in their relationships with each other, with reference to what is good and bad, and what affects the rights and well-being of others."

When we apply these principles to specific circumstances or decisions and act according to what is good rather than what is evil, we are practicing that which is ethical. In other words, *ethics* refers to principles and *ethical* refers to practical behavior. In this book I will use the phrase **what is ethical** to focus on the actual practice of correct behavior. As we all learn and practice what is ethical, we can avoid offending others, enjoy good relationships, and have the satisfaction of living a life respected by wise men and God.

When we speak of ethics, we are referring to the divine laws that God established to define what is right in reference to social behavior. We are not specifically referring to doctrinal truths. Obviously, the only doctrinal truth that exists is what God teaches. This means that both true doctrines and false doctrines exist. We do not have the right to make up our own doctrine. If our doctrine is what God teaches, it is true. Otherwise, it is false. However, when there are doctrinal differences, we are still governed by the laws of God that are related to behavior. At all times and with all people, we must do what is ethical.

God gave us examples to illustrate the difference between beliefs and behavior. In Romans 14, God teaches us that some may differ in their respect for a particular day as opposed to other days, but their behavior must demonstrate respect and not condemnation toward others. He also teaches us that one person's conscience may be different from another's in terms of foods or other things, but his conduct must demonstrate consideration for others and not just for his own opinion.

Jude 22, 23 tells us that even when there is a case of abominable sin, our behavior must still be governed by what is ethical.[1] Today, some Christians, even godly pastors and workers, believe their defense of doctrinal truth gives them reason to sacrifice the principles of God related to behavior. That idea is wrong. It is never right to justify behavior that is unethical. Disregarding one law of God in order to defend another law of God is not God's way, and the person who does so loses his credibility.

Why is there not more effort to define what is ethical and apply the principles to our social experiences? The answer to this question involves the lack of reflection and clear teaching on the subject. Teaching material about ethics is scarce, so many do not have this foundation when making decisions or reacting to circumstances. They may not disagree with what is ethical; they have simply not thought about it. Because of this, they do not consider what is ethical when making decisions or facing those circumstances.

Also, some Christians do not want to be bound by ethical principles. The question of what is ethical does not seem important enough to restrict them in their quest to achieve or gain something. They have acted against their conscience until their

---

[1] *And of some have compassion, making a difference: And others save with fear, pulling them out of the fire; hating even the garment spotted by the flesh* (Jude 22, 23)

ability to discern between good and evil is diminished. They consider their desires and point of view important enough to justify violating what is ethical.

If others do not want to abide by ethical principles in every relationship and situation, why should we establish these rules and abide by them? One reason is so that those who agree that these are important biblical principles might experience the satisfaction and joy of harmony and respect. We want to be part of the solution and not the problem. Otherwise, conflict, rampant corruption, and anarchy can destroy our families, churches, and our faith. Practicing what is ethical is our hope for something better.

More important than the desire for harmony and respect is the deeper sense of personal, spiritual dignity. Noah Webster's first definition of dignity describes this virtue as *"True honor; nobleness or elevation of mind, consisting in a high sense of propriety, truth and justice, with an abhorrence of mean and sinful actions; opposed to meanness. In this sense, we speak of the dignity of mind, and dignity of sentiments."*[2] This personal *"dignity of mind, and dignity of sentiments"* is like a higher plane of life. When we come to know and appreciate the higher ground of God's ways, no other way of life is worthy of living. There is never a reason to sacrifice our spiritual dignity, in spite of what others may think is more convenient or reasonable.

At one time, in the book of 1 Samuel, David and his men hid in a cave in the wilderness of Engedi. King Saul had become corrupt, and God had ordained David to be anointed king. Instead of accepting the will of God, Saul looked for David to kill him. Unaware that David and his men were in the cave, Saul also went in to rest. David's men told him that God had delivered Saul into his hands and encouraged David to kill him.

---

2   Noah Webster's First Edition of an American Dictionary, 1828, Republished in Facsimile Edition by Foundation for American Christian Education, 1967.

They thought nothing could be more reasonable and convenient. Such an act would be self-defense against an enemy rejected by God himself. They believed it was not by chance, but by the work of God that Saul was now in the hands of David.[3]

David ignored the advice of his men because he did not base his decisions on a circumstance that appeared to be a convenient opportunity from God. His decision to spare Saul's life was based on his personal, spiritual dignity, his convictions of right and wrong based on the divine principles of that higher plane of life. His fear of God made him respect the order that God had established. He did not believe he had the right to change this order. Only God had the right to decide when and how to remove the power and life of Saul. David decided not to touch "the Lord's anointed."[4] This was one of many examples showing why God considered David a man after his own heart and why David thrived and was protected. He practiced what is ethical in humility before God.

In the fourth example in the preface, the members of the school board were focused on the welfare of the school and the legality of their right to sell it and buy another campus. If they had thought as David thought, they would have considered the higher ground of whether the matter was ethical, not just whether it was appropriate or legal. They would not use something that had been purchased by others without taking those people into account. Their focus would have been on their responsibility to God and their ability to carry out the change according to his principles.

(Note: Take into consideration that this book was originally written in Spanish for Christians and churches in Mexico. Due to cultural differences, some situations may not be as common in other countries. However, the principles involved will be applicable to all cultures.)

---

3 1 Samuel 24:3-4.
4 1 Samuel 24:6-7.

Chapter 1

Four Fundamental Principles of Ethics

Humility

The greatest reason for knowing and practicing what is ethical is the humble desire to honor God and be faithful to him. This is the first fundamental principle of ethics. If we are humble like David, we will not expect to make decisions according to our judgment of appearance, convenience, or circumstance. We will recognize God's right to determine how to make decisions and recognize the superiority of God's reason and purpose in each one. We will understand that nothing could be wiser, more appropriate, and more secure than God's way of thinking. For this reason, submitting to God will not be done out of a attitude of sacrifice, but out of a feeling of appreciation and desire for his will.

Is this your attitude? Do you yearn to know God's will in your decisions and social relationships? Do you understand the purity that results from doing God's will and the uncertainty that doing our own will produces? That attitude is the foundation for being able to practice what is ethical.

With an attitude of wise humility before God, we grow in the knowledge of God's way of thinking and in the knowledge of his will. We begin to understand that humility is not only a duty to him, but also to others. Obviously, humility before others is different from the humility shown before God. We will not necessarily submit to the will of others as we do to the will of God. Humility before others is an act of obeying the will of God who does not want us to be proud before others. He wants us to honor them and seek their well-being. We must examine our attitude in any given circumstance, because what is ethical depends on this humility.

Responsibility

The second principle, which is a result of humility, is responsibility. Responsibility primarily refers to the question, *What am I responsible to do?* There are two sides to the answer to that question. Sometimes I am responsible to fulfill an obligation or task. Not to do so would be a violation of what is ethical. Other times I have no right to intervene. I might violate what is ethical by getting involved in something that is not my responsibility. To discern what is ethical in any given situation, I must ask myself, "What am I responsible to do?"

To answer this question we must consider four things. First, responsibility involves giving account to someone in authority. Sometimes no other authority is involved besides God. He has spoken to us through his Word and by the example of his Son, and we are responsible to fulfill these direct commands. In other cases, the authority is someone that God has placed over us, such as government officials, parents, pastors, or bosses.

Sometimes we voluntarily agree to accept the authority of someone such as a teacher or a school official. Other times we are the authority and are responsible for those who are under our command or care. Whatever the case, responsibility related to authority is one of the first considerations in determining the answer to the question, *What am I responsible to do?*

Second, responsibility is related to the fulfillment of some agreement. This agreement can vary a great deal in importance, from a simple appointment, to a life-and-death situation. In any case, an agreement represents our word of honor. Not keeping our word is a violation of what is ethical and results in a loss of personal dignity before the eyes of God and society. God requires that we keep our word.

We must understand two exceptions to this rule that are not very common. We could enter into an agreement that we have no authority to make, and that agreement must be annulled or modified according to the authority whose right is in question. If this happens, we should repent for having acted without the right to do so and take personal responsibility for it.

The other exception occurs when we discover that an agreement will endanger or damage other people who are not involved in the agreement. Then it is necessary to consider the safety of others a priority. If the agreement was a malicious trap, we should feel no shame about annulling it; but if it was made honestly, we must accept responsibility for our actions.

Third, responsibility is related to the quality of our work or efforts. In many cases, this relates to agreements, but not always. One way we might defraud another without breaking our word of honor is to fulfill some agreement with an inferior quality of work or effort. What is ethical is also a matter of quality, and God commands us to produce quality that would be appropriate to present to him.[5]

A lack of quality in the fulfillment of agreements, work, or production may be the result of sloth, irresponsibility, or malice. Whatever the case, it is always a violation of what is ethical. Our dignity depends upon our reputation of being a careful, diligent person who does our best according to what a situation requires.

Fourth, responsibility must be practiced as a habit. It is not a principle that is only applied to certain circumstances; it is a personal character quality that is demonstrated in all aspects

---

[5] Colossians 3:22-25.

of life. When responsibility is a habit, discerning or fulfilling what is ethical is not difficult.

Respect

The third principle that also comes from godly humility and is essential for determining what is ethical is respect. The word *respect* means "to regard another highly or consider another worthy of esteem."

Everyone respects some person, but not always in the way that God teaches. Respect is ethical only if it is felt and demonstrated in humility before God. For example, the apostle James had to reprimand some Christians in his time because they showed respect to the rich but not to the poor.[6] The wrong kind of respect can be a violation of what is ethical.

Practicing the type of respect that God teaches is important. God is not a respecter of persons, nor does he want his children to be so. God regards the rich and the poor alike. Contrary to how the world places value on people, he does not esteem men as worthy of more or less value because of appearance, intelligence, ability, personality, race, family, or nationality. James warned of the error of blessing *God, even the Father,* and cursing *men which are made after the similitude of God.*[7] God sees all men as made in his image, and he loves them so much that he sacrificed his own Son to save them. Likewise, God demands that we value and respect all men.

However, God does make a distinction between the value of a person and the value of his deeds. God loved Cain and Abel equally and made no distinction between them. But he did respect Abel's offering and not Cain's. Noah found favor in the eyes of God, not because of his value as a man, but because of his just deeds. God chose David from among his brothers,

---

6 James 2:1-9.
7 James 3:9-10.

not because of some external quality, but because of his heart. Thus, what is ethical requires a general respect for all men, and a particular respect for those who demonstrate good qualities and righteous hearts.

What do we do about men who practice evil? The same concept applies. Just as God distinguishes between the person and his actions, we must do the same. With discernment and wisdom, a person can show the respect that is commanded toward a person and, at the same time, despise and rebuke the evil which that person commits. Let us not forget that despite the anger which God felt towards the evil of the world, and despite the just, eternal judgment he bestowed upon the world, he showed how much he valued the world. He loved the world and sent his own Son to bear our punishment and save those who believe in him.

Finally, what is ethical not only requires respect for others, but requires being respectable as well. We can rejoice in the fact that God values us, but at the same time, we must show godly qualities – from a just and sincere heart – that are worthy of esteem by God and man.

Protecting What Is Important to God

So far, it has been noted that a humble attitude will produce responsibility and respect in accordance with God's heart. All three of these qualities together will result in the fourth principle: the development of a strong desire to protect what is important to God.

We can understand that God has known us since the day we were born. He observes us each day of our lives and knows our struggles and burdens. God sees how the Devil and the world deceive and corrupt us in order to destroy us. God wants us to know the truth and be saved from corruption and condemnation.

ETHICAL

Being aware of how important humanity is to God, we should feel responsible to do whatever we can to fulfill God's desires.

This allows us to realize how much God loves his children and his desire is to see us take an active part in the local church, as part of the body of Christ. Therefore, we no longer have the "each to his own" attitude, but rather feel responsible to protect God's children from what could undermine what God wants for us. Naturally, our spiritual integrity is important to God, so practicing what is ethical fulfills God's commandment to *consider one another to provoke unto love and to good works.*[8] The irritation we may feel from another's mistakes or whims is no longer just a bother, but becomes a concern for the well-being of the body. Another person's mistakes motivate us to be an example of spiritual integrity and create a desire in us to encourage integrity in the lives of others.

Protecting the welfare of what God loves is not restricted to spiritual welfare. If we are ethical, we have compassion toward the emotional and physical needs of others. We make an effort to procure harmony and unity in the church, because God wants his church to *keep the unity of the Spirit in the bond of peace.*[9] Division and disharmony are grave dangers to the church, and the issues that cause them are not always as important as God's desire for his children to function as healthy members of one harmonious body.

We should note the significance of the home in protecting what is important to God. The family is the "brick" with which the church is built. God created marriage and the family, and most of his children's spiritual edification and care is fulfilled in the home.

A healthy church depends on healthy families. Therefore, protection of what is important to God is also centered on the

---
8   Hebrews 10:24.
9   Ephesians 4:3.

well-being of the family. We should endeavor to achieve order, respect, and love within marriages according to the wisdom and commandments of God. Fostering a better understanding between parents and children will serve to accomplish these spiritual, emotional, intellectual, and physical purposes.

Thus, we find that practicing what is ethical depends on four character qualities. The most important of these qualities is humility – denying ourselves and seeking the will of God and the well-being of others. Humility produces two other qualities – the responsibility of knowing and doing our part and the feeling of respect for others. The fourth quality is a result of the first three – the desire to protect God's children from threats to their spiritual integrity and harmony in the church and in the home.

To practice what is ethical is to apply these qualities to situations where we could do what is not ethical. Naming all such situations is not possible. However, we can name some of the most common situations and give examples of how to practice what is ethical. By knowing the principles that determine what is ethical, we can transform our thinking to help us discern what is ethical in any situation.

Chapter 2

Knowing When to Obey or Counter Authority

Authority is an important area in which we must practice what is ethical. God established authority and has commanded us to respect authorities. Because of this, our respect for authority shows our obedience to and respect for God himself. All of us are under different authorities in different circumstances. To practice what is ethical first requires that we know who our authorities are and what the responsibilities are that we have toward each of them. Only God has universal authority. The other authorities that he has established are limited to certain relationships and circumstances.

For instance, God has placed a wife under the authority of both her husband and her pastor. However, a wife's responsibilities toward these two authorities are different. Her husband has no authority to tell her to collect the offerings at the church on a Sunday, and the pastor has no authority to tell her how to discipline the children. There is an order in each relationship of authority, and doing what is ethical depends on respecting this order.

In many cases, a chain of command exists. At home, children are under the authority of their mother and father, and the mother is under the authority of her husband. If a mother gives instructions to her children, they will be responsible for carrying out these instructions. If they decide not to pay attention to her and appeal to their father, they are out of order and are not doing what is ethical. If the mother receives instructions from her husband concerning a task for her children, and she does not obey her husband but changes his instructions against his will, she is out of order, and she is not doing what is ethical. Obviously, all of these instructions must be within God's will, or the parents themselves are out of order.

Bypassing an Authority

We see, then, that one of the concepts of doing what is ethical is respecting the chain of command. Bypassing authorities and not respecting their positions and responsibilities is not ethical. Knowing the chain of command is important. In some cases, this chain is directly taught in the Bible. In other cases, an "organizational chart" of authority may exist at church, at work, at school, or in the government. In every case, to do what is ethical we must respect and follow this order.

A lack of ethical behavior is too common in this area. Ignoring the chain of command happens at church when we think a higher authority will respond more favorably than the immediate one. For instance, a person may ask the pastor for permission to sing a solo instead of asking the music director who is in charge of special music. A family may ask the pastor for permission to have a youth activity at their house instead of first consulting the youth director. A child who is not given permission from a parent to get a cup from the kitchen may ask the other parent, in the hope of a positive response.

Sometimes this involves taking advantage of a family relationship with an authority. Even worse, the motivation might have something to do with what the immediate authority knows that the highest authority does not. This problem happens at work and undermines the order and purposes of authorities that God has established.

The exception to the rule occurs when, after receiving

instructions from an authority, it is clear that fulfilling these instructions would be a violation of the wishes of higher authorities. In this case, the ethical response would be to appeal to the immediate authority to reconsider the instructions that have been given, taking into account the higher authority's desire. If the immediate authority does not pay attention to the higher authority, the immediate authority will be out of order. In this case, appealing to the higher authority for instructions would not be unethical. On the contrary, it could be a violation of what is ethical not to protect the interests of the higher authority.

In a business that I once owned, a supervisor was in charge of the workers. Her responsibility was to make sure all the workers fulfilled their duties. However, on occasion, she would change the work schedule for some personal convenience and would also allow the workers to consume our product without paying for it. She would tell them, "Don't say anything to Pastor Morris." In these cases, the workers should have appealed to her to be honest and to allow them to be honest also. If that did not correct the problem, they should have informed me of the situation.

In the situations described, there are also extremes that must be avoided. The cases in which it not ethical follow the instructions of an immediate authority must be serious. Jesus Christ warned that it is an error to *strain at a gnat, and swallow a camel*.[10] Any authority has a certain flexibility to make decisions and give instructions that might not be exactly what the higher authority would have done in every detail. This is necessary for efficiency and smoothness of order and is not against the most important desires of the higher authorities. In these cases, we must respect the immediate authority and trust the higher authority to make any necessary changes.

The other extreme is an attitude of indifference when we know

---

10 Matthew 23:24.

we are being instructed to do something that could undermine what is important to the higher authorities. The Bible depicts several examples in which obedience to an immediate authority would have been a serious disobedience to God, who is the maximum authority.

One case was the disobedience of Shadrach, Meshach, and Abednego to Nebuchadnezzar's command to bow before an idol.[11] They had respected the authority of this king in spite of the fact that he was a pagan, he had destroyed the land of Israel, and he had taken captive its inhabitants. So important is the fact that God has established authority, that even under this cruel king, they had served faithfully and responsibly to a level of excellence. However, when the king gave a command that was against God's authority and was a serious violation of God's will, these men recognized their obligation to respect God's command first and face the consequences of being burned to death.

In the same way, Peter and John disobeyed their immediate authority when they were told to quit preaching and teaching in Jesus' name, which was directly against Jesus' command. They practiced this exception to the rule by saying it is necessary *to obey God rather than men.*[12] However, we must recognize that these exceptions are few. In most situations, these men had submitted and been respectful toward their immediate authorities in spite of the fact that these authorities were not faithful to God.

The experiences of two women illustrate the need to consider the seriousness of the situation. Abraham asked Sarah on two different occasions to hide the fact that she was his wife. He told her to say that she was his sister so the people of the land they were visiting would not kill him to take her as a wife. Although

---

11   Daniel 3.
12   Acts 4:19-20; 5:29.

must have appeared to be devious, she understood that respect for the authority of her husband was the most important issue in this case. She may have recognized the special relationship that he had with God.

On the other hand, Abigail saw that the will of her husband was against the will of God. She knew he would cause the death of others and create a stain on the reputation of the man that God had anointed as king. Because of this, she acted against the will of her husband, taking food to David and pleading with him not to damage the reputation that would be important to him as king.

Sometimes discerning when not to obey the commands of an authority is difficult. God always looks on the heart. He desires to see a true respect for the authority and order that he has established. He expects to see attempts to resolve difficult cases without disobedience to an immediate authority. This occurred in the example of Daniel when he sought an alternative to fulfill the king's purpose, while not violating God's will by eating forbidden foods.[13]

Authority must be taken seriously. A flippant attitude about disobedience, using the excuse of having to "obey God," is a violation of what is ethical and becomes an act of pride instead of humility.

Interfering With an Authority

Just as bypassing an authority is a violation of what is ethical, so also is interfering in the exercise of the authority's responsibility. Since an authority will give account to his superiors and to God for the correct or incorrect use of his position, he has a certain right to make decisions according to his own criteria.

An authority has to consider many things when making his decisions. He must not only be concerned about his subordinates'

---

13   Daniel 1:8-13.

work and responsibilities, but also about his relationship with them. His decisions will affect his reputation, his capability to lead, and the attitudes and discipline of his workers. Taking away an authority's right to evaluate and make decisions by his own criteria when he will be responsible is a violation of what is ethical.

A common example of interfering with an authority in a church is when we have an idea for a project, event, or activity that should be approved by a higher authority, including the pastor. Many times we comment about or promote our idea with other people or with some group with which the higher authority is ministering. Finally, after building excitement and expectation in the minds and emotions of others, we present our idea to the authority who must give approval. Now, however, this authority can no longer make an objective decision according to his criteria and responsibility, because the emotions and expectations of people are predisposed toward completion of the idea.

The authority may want to deny approval of the idea due to a previous experience, a conflict with another event, a difference in priorities, or the character of the person promoting the idea. However, if he does not approve the idea, he knows people will react to the rejection of something they are expecting. This can result in discontentment or bad feelings, and might affect his relationships, or cause a conflict with those relationships in the future.

Often an authority will feel obligated to approve something to prevent bad feelings, even though he believes it will result in negative consequences. His right to make the decision has been taken away due to interference in the order that God has established. If we have an idea that needs approval by some authority, we should present the idea to the authority before discussing it with anyone else. This way, we can receive instruction about whether or not it can be completed and receive procedures to follow if the authority agrees. Only then should we begin to present our idea to other people.

An example of what happens when this principle is not followed is described in the preface of this book (see page IX). In that situation, a pastor offered a job to a secretary from another pastor's church and afterwards asked the other pastor for a recommendation. A desire to do what is ethical would have motivated him to speak to the other pastor before offering a job to the secretary. Then he could have asked for both his recommendation and blessing.

That would have allowed for a serious recommendation, and, with a more complete understanding, the first pastor could have decided to invite the secretary to work or not. In addition, the other pastor would have gained more respect for him after seeing his wisdom in knowing and practicing what is ethical.

Many parents have had a similar experience with their children. A child will ask his parents for permission to do something with another family when that family is present. The parents could have a reason to deny permission to their child. Perhaps they had other plans, or perhaps the child has not earned the right because of a lack of obedience. There may even be concern about a lack of wisdom, character, or safe conditions with the other family.

However, now the question was asked in the presence of the other family. Due to their fear of offending or causing hard feelings, an interference exists in the way that they would normally make the decision. Children must be taught about what is ethical in these situations. They should be obligated to ask permission in private to avoid possible conflicts and not remove the right of their parents to make decisions in all freedom.

A biblical example of this interference with an authority is seen when the people of Capernaum asked Peter, *Doth not your master pay tribute?* This tribute was a temple tax.

Peter did not take into account Jesus' right to respond to this situation according to his own criteria and answered, *Yes.* On this hasty response, Spurgeon comments "Peter was in such a hurry to vindicate his Lord that he compromised him. "He saith, Yes." He might have asked his Lord's mind, or he might have referred the collectors to Jesus himself; but he was in a hurry, and thought himself safe enough in maintaining his Master's reputation. He was quite certain that his Lord would do all that good people did. Our Savior and his cause have often suffered from the zeal of friends. Christ is better known by what he says himself than by what his friends say for him."[14]

When he returned, Jesus asked, *What thinkest thou, Simon? of whom do the kings of the earth take custom or tribute? of their own children, or of strangers?*

Peter responded, *Of strangers.*

Jesus said, *Then are the children free.*[15]

Although there was no money and he was not rightfully obligated to pay this fee, Jesus made a decision to pay, miraculously, just for the purpose of not offending the people or damaging his relationship with them. However, Peter learned his lesson, that he had overstepped his authority and spoken out of turn. We would be wise to learn the same lesson in ethics and give authorities the right to their own response.

Separate Chains of Command

Other situations when it is important to consider what is ethical involve two different authorities. Each one represents a separate chain of command, and confusion or conflict can occur if the two chains use the same people. This happens when

---

14 Spurgeon's Commentary on Matthew.
15 Matthew 17:24-26.

one authority seeks help from a person who is under another authority without the other's approval. The problem is obvious. If the second authority already has plans, purposes, and instructions for the people under him, but one of his people is working for another, the second authority will either not be able to fulfill his responsibilities or will have to interfere with those of the first authority. What is ethical in this situation is for one authority always to ask permission of the other when seeking help from a person who is under his direction.

Even worse than the organizational problems, the lack of practicing what is ethical between two authorities may also damage the loyalty of people and cause division. Any relationship between an authority and the people under his direction not only implies responsibility but also loyalty.

A wise authority will attempt to win the trust of his people in order to develop loyalty and establish a better relationship to fulfill his purposes. If another authority gets involved with these people, issues of communication, personality, methods, experience, and feelings can affect this loyalty.

Sometimes people do this out of ignorance about what is ethical and about the damage that may result. In the worst cases, this is done purposely to rob loyalty from another for one's own benefit. Absalom did this to his father, David.[16] He manipulated the feelings of the people to *[steal] their hearts* and later used that loyalty against David. Few things are more despicable than this and will surely result in disgrace, as was the case for Absalom. Proverbs 6:19 says that sowing *discord among brethren* is something that God hates. Whether it is done on purpose or through ignorance or carelessness, this can cause great damage. We must practice what is ethical in situations which involve loyalty to an authority.

One example of a violation of what is ethical in matters

---
16   2 Samuel 15:1-6.

of authority is when an ex-pastor visits people who had been under his care. There are always differences in personalities, methods, and philosophies of ministry. If the ex-pastor gives an unfavorable opinion about something the new pastor is doing, he will damage the loyalty of the people toward their pastor and could sow discord.

What is ethical in these cases is to ask permission first of the present pastor to visit the people and then respect the decision that he makes. If permission is given, he must take much care not to sow discord. If he sees something that is not biblical, he must discuss it only with the present pastor.

Consider the case of the pastor mentioned in the preface (see page IX) who visited a family in the church he had pastored. If he had first asked permission from the present pastor and had focused on God's purpose to use that pastor to edify his flock, he would have avoided talking about any negative issue. He could have strengthened the confidence the family had in God's purpose to use their pastor to edify them. The result would have been greater unity in the church, greater spiritual growth, and greater respect between the two pastors.

The exception to this rule is when a pastor is practicing something that is unbiblical or immoral, and will not listen to another pastor's attempts to restore him to faithfulness before God. Then the people of the church must not be left exposed to spiritual danger, and a solution must be sought. The case of the apostle John and Diotrephes is a biblical example of this exception.[17] A person must be careful, however, not to use this exception as an excuse to justify some act that in reality has no spiritual or biblical basis.

Another example of interference occurs between families. Parents must fulfill the responsibilities they have toward their children even when it is not enjoyable. They work to provide

---

17   3 John 9-11.

for their children and care for them. They sacrifice when their children are ill or hurt, and they strive to give them education and preparation for life. This means that their relationship with their children is not always fun and games. Parents must also correct and discipline their children during the years in which they are maturing.

When children are with their friend's parents, things are not the same. These adults do not have the heavy responsibilities that the children's parents have. They can spend their time showing hospitality and providing affection, fun, and games. An immature child may be ignorant of all that his own parents do for him and not appreciate the sacrifices they make. He may feel bad about discipline and correction, without discerning the love and benefits involved. He is only aware that when he is with the other family, he finds happiness, fun, and affection without all the tasks, responsibilities, and discipline that he experiences at home.

This is a normal situation and is often inevitable. It is not harmful, but rather part of the process of maturing if the other parents practice what is ethical. They should always build appreciation, love, and respect in the child toward his own parents. This child's parents should also know and respect the standards and desires that the other parents have toward their children.

Unfortunately, this situation sometimes lends itself to what is not ethical. Some parents "steal the hearts" of others' children. Instead of correcting complaints that a child has toward his parents, they feel superior or better in some way. With such attitudes, or because of a lack of Christian maturity, they may think they know better than the other parents and not respect their standards and desires. They justify themselves because they do not directly speak against the parents of the child, but rather speak well of them. However, their tone of voice tells the child there is negligence in his home.

Sometimes a family might promote a romantic relationship which the other parents have no knowledge of and would not approve of. In the end, instead of building unity with the child and his parents, they build barriers, resentment, and pain. This practice is not only unethical; it is damaging and despicable.

Conscious Abuse

The worst case of an ethical violation with authority is the conscious and purposeful abuse of a position of authority to achieve personal benefit or gain. This abuse occurs in politics, business, and even in the church. Some pastors and church authorities take advantage of the people financially and even dip into the treasury.

In other cases, the benefit they seek is power, and "anything goes" in order to gain it. They know how to use sweet flattery as well as subtle criticism to manipulate others. Secret meetings are the clearest violation of what is ethical. They are considered useful, however, because what is ethical is seen as a weakness.

Some of these church authorities are wolves dressed as sheep.[18] Others are believers who have fallen into pride, vanity, and greed. They cause divisions, resentment, and dishonor to the way of truth. At the same time, they present themselves as *ministers of righteousness*. They speak with sweetness and kindness, but *Their throat is an open sepulchre; with their tongues they have used deceit; the poison of asps is under their lips*.[19] The people think they are their friends, not knowing they are only being used.

When a spiritual member with the spirit of meekness[20] attempts to restore such a person to honesty and self-denial, he is

---

18   Matthew 7:15.
19   Romans 3:13.
20   Galatians 6:1.

only cast aside or defamed. May God deliver us from those who appear as *angel[s] of light* but are deceitful ministers of Satan.[21]

We must reject what is done in secret and rebuke that which does not edify but destroys. Greed must be detected and corrected or eliminated. To permit the subtle manipulations of church authorities is to be an accomplice to their carnal works.

There are other examples of ethical and non-ethical practice in relation to authority, but we cannot name them all. I have described the principles of what is ethical, with examples, so any reader can understand and apply them to any situation. This is necessary to walk in wisdom and achieve well-being in the family, the church, and the lives of others.

---

21 2 Corinthians 11:14-15.

Chapter 3

Ethical Treatment of Things We Don't Own

Ethical concerns are not only important in matters of authority but also in regard to the possessions of others. In life, many experiences will test whether or not we practice what is ethical. When it comes to possessions, our ethical behavior is often lacking.

Some friends were discussing what kind of car is best for traveling on a very bad road. Several suggested various brands, naming certain qualities of those brands. Suddenly, one friend interrupted the conversation and stated authoritatively, "I know exactly what car is best for traveling on a very bad road – a borrowed car."

Of course, he was joking, but the joke was based on a real problem involving the lack of ethics when people use or borrow items from other people. God gave his people many instructions regarding the use of other people's possessions. The three chapters following the Ten Commandments in Exodus mention this responsibility.

God told his people that if someone dug a well and didn't cover it, and someone else's ox or donkey fell into the well, the person who dug the well would have to pay the owner of the ox or donkey for his loss.[22] In this way, God made people responsible to think about and care for the possessions of others. He

---

22 Exodus 21:33-34.

made them financially responsible if their lack of responsibility resulted in harm to another's property.

God also said that if someone's ox killed another's ox, the dead ox should be divided between both owners, the live one sold, and the money divided equally. In this case, the level of responsibility was less, and they shared the loss. But God said that if the owner of the ox knew his animal was violent and didn't keep it in, he would have to keep the dead ox and the owner of the dead ox would be able to keep the live ox.[23]

Later, God said that if one person's animal ate from another's field, the owner of the animal would pay for the loss.[24] Again we see that a person is responsible for the proper care of another's possessions. God also said that if someone started a fire, and it burned another's harvest field, the one who started the fire must pay for the loss.

After this, God said that if someone was taking care of another's possession as a favor to that person and that possession was stolen, or in the case of an animal, if it died, the person should be judged to see if he was caring for it responsibly. If he was caring for the possession responsibly, he would be innocent. But if he stole it, or even if it was stolen as a result of his negligence, he would pay for the loss.[25]

God said that even if someone finds an enemy's possession, he should take it back to him.[26] In the book of Leviticus, we find instructions about the responsibility a person has regarding another's possessions. God said a person should not hold the wages of a worker past his payday and he should be honest in matters of buying and selling.[27]

In Deuteronomy, God commanded his people not to move

---

23 Exodus 21:35-36.
24 Exodus 22:5.
25 Exodus 22:7-12.
26 Exodus 23:4.
27 Leviticus 19:13.

the landmarks for property limits but to respect the property of another.[28] Then, he said a person could eat the fruit or corn in another's field if the person was hungry, but he could not take any with him in a basket or bag.[29] God repeated his commandment to return a lost item to its owner, adding that if the owner was not known, he should keep the possession until the owner came looking for it.[30]

Because of these examples, we can establish that it is important to God how we treat others' possessions. This plays a key role in defining what is ethical. We can apply the four fundamental principles of what is ethical: humility, responsibility, respect, and protection. Since God cares how we treat the possessions of others, in humility we will exercise more care for their possessions than we will for our own.

This is diametrically opposed to the belief that is common in the world and in human nature. Those in the world do not have a sense of what is ethical. They tend to value what belongs to them and disrespect what belongs to others. In this case, the example of the borrowed car is not simply a joke. The owner of the car would probably be more careful to clean the mud from his shoes before entering, more careful not to scratch the paint or stain the interior, more careful to avoid harm during the trip, and more careful to keep it safe when not in use. Sometimes, unfortunately, we are not as careful as we should be, since we will not be suffering from the effects of the loss.

It is not ethical to exert less care when using another's property. Some people even fail to care for their own property. Even though they have this right, they do not have the right when it comes to another's property.

---

28 Deuteronomy 19:14.
29 Deuteronomy 23:24-25.
30 Deuteronomy 22:1-2.

The Use of Public Property

Ethical use of the possessions of others must be applied to a variety of circumstances. For example, it should be applied when we are given permission to use a home, vehicle, or other property. It also applies to public facilities such as churches, public buildings, parks, or walkways.

One example of the abuse of public property is in public restrooms. The following story describes a situation that is too common in some areas of the world. Right before the church service started, a man ran to the bathroom with a cup of coffee in his hand. He didn't put the toilet seat up, and while using the toilet, he spilled his coffee. Not only was the toilet seat left dirty, but the floor as well.

I'm sure they have someone who cleans the church, he reasoned.

While he was washing his hands, he bumped the cup he had placed on the sink and splashed coffee all over the sink and wall. Fortunately for him, no one was looking, and since it was already late, he left his mess and hurried to the auditorium. Soon after, another man who was visiting entered the men's restroom. The condition of the restroom left him with a bad impression of the church.

During the rest of his visit, this negative impression caused him to notice other ways the service and people failed to meet his expectations. The people were kind, but he was not sure he would return.

How uncomfortable it is to enter a restroom where people with no sense of what is ethical have been. Some stain the seats and the floor and don't bother to clean up after themselves. Others leave the bathroom dirty, steal toilet paper, write on the walls, and leave the water running in the sink.

If we have a fundamental sense of what is ethical, we will think about pleasing God and respecting others. We will leave the restroom in the same condition we found it or better. And, of course, we will not take what is not ours. If the man in the story had been thinking about the well-being of others and honoring the Lord, he would have been more careful about not soiling the restroom and would have taken time to clean up after himself. This would have changed the first impression that the visitor experienced, and his outlook regarding the church could have been completely different.

It is amazing and unfortunate that even in the house of God we find an abuse of what is ethical. Besides public restrooms, we can also find pews, benches, and chairs stained, scratched, or broken because of a lack of respect for God's property. Some people even do these things on purpose. Gum under the chair or on the floor is another example of this kind of abuse.

Parents allow their children to leave trash, write on walls, and ruin furniture, gardens, and even vehicles that belong to others without taking responsibility for what their children have done. This is not only a lack of ethics, but blatant irreverence toward God himself. Since what is ethical is based mainly on humility before God, in God's house there should be a greater sense of respect, responsibility, and protection.

There are many other examples. If people practiced what is ethical, we would not have a problem with trash in the streets, harm done to plants, or graffiti on walls. How much better our environment and our circumstances would be if there was a profound sense of what is ethical.

The Use of Rented Items

The second area in which we must be ethical regarding other people's property concerns the use of rented items. This involves an agreement where two or more people accept responsibility in relation to a possession for the benefit of both parties. The agreement can be a specific written or verbal contract, or it could be part of a cultural understanding.

When we rent or ask to borrow someone else's possession, we are entering into an agreement which must be understood and respected. It is not ethical to break or change the conditions of the agreement without the knowledge and consent of the other party. An agreement can only be changed by a new agreement.

If we rent a property, building, house, car, furniture, or other item, we benefit, but so does the owner. For example, the owner of a home expects to receive his rent money and to receive his house back in reasonably good condition by the date agreed upon. We expect to have a place to live, work, rest, and go about our daily life without buying the house. The conditions of this agreement include money, the due date for the rent, appropriate care (taking into consideration normal wear and tear), and the keeping of the conditions under which the rent agreement was made.

Certain incorrect changes in this agreement are obvious. The landlord doesn't have the right to demand the rent money before the due date. We do not have the right to keep the rent money past the due date. The landlord does not have the right to raise the rent without previous notice. We do not have the right to give less than what is right during that time. The landlord does not have the right to throw a party in the house. We do not have the right to remodel the house without the consent of the owner.

Other changes in the agreement are not as obvious. The matter of normal wear and tear is one of these. What may seem to be normal wear and tear to one person can look like a disaster to another. Some things can be restored to their original condition, such as walls that can be painted. Other items cannot be as easily restored, as in the case of carpet, windows, or broken lamps. Normal wear and tear is not unethical, but abuse and misuse of property is.

Sometimes the problem may not be a case of breaking or

changing an agreement, but of causing expectations that cannot honestly be fulfilled. For example, if we rent out a house on a peaceful Saturday, knowing that a train passes nearby every two hours on the other days of the week, which we don't mention to the tenant, we are being dishonest and acting unethically.

On the other hand, the prospective tenant may have unrealistic expectations regarding the conditions of the house. If we warn the tenant about the train, and he believes it will not be a problem but decides later that he does not like the noise, he cannot blame us. If he accuses us of acting unethically or refuses to pay the rent and take care of the house, he is the one who is being unethical.

Practicing the four fundamental principles of ethics in the matter of rental agreements will eliminate all lack of honesty, avoid unrealistic and unmet expectations, and only allow the agreement to be changed when both parties consent.

Use of Borrowed Items

Using borrowed items is similar to matters involving rented items. The difference, however, is that since the only person receiving a benefit is the person borrowing the item, he has a greater responsibility to return the item on time and in the same condition in which he received it. When we ask to borrow an item, we should be conscientious of the responsibility involved and diligently practice what is ethical.

Receiving a benefit without having to pay should motivate us to be grateful for the kindness and consideration that the owner is showing. It should also motivate us to show gratitude by making sure that the item is not damaged, and by respecting the time frame given for borrowing and returning it. If we forget or are negligent in returning a borrowed item on time or fail to abide by the conditions agreed upon, we should accept the blame for not acting correctly, ask for forgiveness, and be responsible for any damage done.

If we borrowed something like food, gas, or some other consumable item, we need to understand and honor the expectations of the owner. Sometimes we return the same quantity as was used. Doing what is ethical requires that any small difference between what was received and what is left to return should be more, rather than less. Other times the owner does not expect to receive the amount that was used. This means that it was not actually borrowed but given as a gift. In those cases, our gratitude should be displayed by showing appreciation, loyalty, or the willingness to return the favor in the future.

A similar situation could involve lending an object to be returned along with a consumable item. This could be something as large as a car with gasoline or a house with gas, electricity, and water. On the other hand, it could be something as small as a dish with food. Whether large or small, expensive or inexpensive, what really matters is the practice of what is ethical, which will determine the worth of our word of honor as well as our personal character. Because of this, any borrowed object is significant and should be cared for as something of great importance.

Sometimes we know the owner is a kind and understanding person, has few expectations, and accepts loss without becoming resentful. To abuse the kindness of such a person is all the more sad, ungrateful, and unethical.

Taking advantage of the kindness of others and not abiding by an agreement is opposite of what it should be. If a lender is kind, we should feel more responsible to meet the conditions of the agreement, not less. God has determined that we will reap the kindness that we sow and that we should show honor to whom honor is due. God will not take lightly abuse committed against those who show great kindness.

Of course, many times the kindness of a person is shown in the flexibility and opportunity he allows within an agreement. Enjoying this flexibility and kindness is not an abuse of ethics, because it is part of the actual agreement. Even in this case, however, ethics requires that we appreciate the person showing the kindness and care for the borrowed item with diligence and gratefulness.

Since the matter of borrowed items involves agreements, we need to consider what is ethical when changing agreements. This is different from the case we previously analyzed involving rented items. The difference is that the owner does not receive any benefit in the agreement to lend an item and is therefore not giving up any rights. He has the right, for example, to change the agreement according to his will and preference, and the person borrowing the item must respect this right. Because of this, proper ethics requires that if we borrow an item, we must accept that the lender is in complete control of the agreement. As the borrower, we must respect any change that the lender makes to the agreement.

However, if we lend a consumable product that cannot be replenished immediately, we cannot expect the borrower to do so until it is possible. Also, ethics requires the borrower to submit to the lender, but this does not give the lender license to ignore any hardship the borrower may suffer if the agreement is changed.

Violations of ethics are common when they involve borrowed money. God's instructions to a person lending money are different from his instructions to a person borrowing money. Matthew 5:42 says, *Give to him that asketh thee, and from him that would borrow of thee turn not thou away.* Whereas Proverbs 22:7 says, *The rich ruleth over the poor, and the borrower is servant to the lender.* It is clear that if someone is able to lend, God is interested in kindness and compassion. But, God warns of the danger of borrowing as something to be avoided.

This difference is also expressed in the law of Moses. One of the blessings promised to the Israelites for being obedient and faithful was the ability to lend, rather than the need to borrow. Deuteronomy 15:5-6 says, *Only if thou carefully hearken unto the voice of the LORD thy God, to observe to do all these commandments which I command thee this day. For the LORD thy God blesseth thee, as he promised thee: and thou shalt lend unto many nations, but thou shalt not borrow; and thou shalt reign over many nations, but they shall not reign over thee.* Notice how God relates the matter of lending to being in power. God does not want his people to be under the dominion of others, and borrowing results in coming under this kind of dominion.

When God warned his people of the curse that would result from disobedience and unfaithfulness, he said, *The stranger that is within thee shall get up above thee very high; and thou shalt come down very low. He shall lend to thee, and thou shalt not lend to him: he shall be the head, and thou shalt be the tail.*[31] Although God desires his people to be kind and compassionate in lending to the needy, he does not want his people to form the habit of borrowing from others.

Although God speaks of the need to borrow as the fruit of disobedience, he does not say that borrowing in itself is a sin. He warns that the act of borrowing places a person in danger of sinning. Psalm 37:21 says, *The wicked borroweth, and payeth not again: but the righteous sheweth mercy, and giveth.* In paying or not paying what is owed, we practice what is or is not ethical.

In many circumstances, what is ethical in borrowing money is no different from what is ethical in borrowing other items. An agreement establishes conditions, which may include how the money is used, how the money will be returned, when the

---

31 Deuteronomy 28:43-44.

money will be returned, and whether interest is to be paid. Certain rights are involved, and these rights involve the benefits each person in the agreement is to receive, each person's word of honor, and the possibilities that exist in the agreement.

Applying the fundamental elements of what is ethical to this situation – humility, responsibility, respect, and protection – we conclude that we should respect the purpose for which the money was borrowed. If the agreement did not mention any specific use of the money, then we have the liberty to use the money as we see fit within the boundaries of what is ethical. If the money was lent for a specific purpose, then we do not have the right to use the money for any other purpose. Once again, the only correct way to change an agreement is to replace it with another agreement.

Some time ago, a man needed money and wanted to sell an old baby grand piano that was stored at a friend's house in another city. However, the piano was broken and needed to be repaired. This man asked me to lend him money to repair and sell the piano. The agreement was that he would repay me first and meet his need with the rest.

Several months went by. I happened to be in the town where this man's friend had stored the piano, so I went to visit him. To my surprise, the piano had not been repaired or even moved. Besides this, his friend was annoyed because the piano occupied a large space in his living room, and no one had been sent to pick it up. When I confronted the man to whom I had lent the money, he told me that he spent the money on something else. This is a classic example of the violation of what is ethical involving the agreed-upon use for borrowed money.

Also, when a person abuses what is ethical in one way, he often abuses it in other ways as well. This man not only violated what is ethical regarding how the money was to be used; he also failed to respect the time frame agreed upon and the way in which the money was to be returned.

When individuals change the time and the way borrowed money is to be returned, at their own convenience, they take away the lender's right to decide what to do with his own money. They act as if they have the exclusive right to use the money in any way they choose and the right to decide how and where to return the money. In most cases, if the one who showed kindness by lending money knew beforehand he would be treated with such disdain, he would not have lent them anything. This proves an element of deceit exists when there is a violation of what is ethical in this area.

If we value dignity and integrity, and desire to have a good name and reputation, we need to consider the following principles and rules when receiving borrowed money. First, borrowed money is not our own. It is the same as any other borrowed item – it belongs to the owner. We can have the benefit of using it to accomplish the purpose agreed upon for the time agreed upon, but it is not ours and we have no right to it. We do not have the right to use it for any other purpose. The owner alone has that right. We do not have the right to use it after the deadline agreed upon. When the time comes to return the money, it belongs to the owner, and he alone has the right to do whatever he wants with it.

Some try to avoid being subject to this principle by reasoning that the owner's money has already been used and the money they now have is money that belongs to them. Try using that reasoning when the owner is a bank with a lender contract and you will see how mistaken it is.

According to law, when the deadline agreed upon in a bank loan comes, the money no longer belongs to the one who borrowed it. If we believe it belongs to us and don't return the money, both our money and other possessions can be seized in order to force us to return the money that belongs to the bank. There is no difference between the right of the bank and the right of any other person who lends money. It is only easier to take advantage of someone who lends money as a matter of trust and without a contract, or is too kind or too embarrassed to take the matter to the authorities. How sad that even the church of God could take advantage of others because doing so seems easy and without consequences.

If we have borrowed money and the time comes to pay it, any money that we have up to the amount borrowed does not belong to us but rather to the owner. In that moment, only the owner has the right to decide what to do with his own money. We could appeal to the owner for an extension of the deadline or a change in the agreement, but the owner has the right to decide what to do with what belongs to him.

We do not have the right to use the money to eat or pay utilities such as rent, electricity, and water, because that would be like robbing money from another to pay for these needs. No matter what, doing what is ethical requires that we accept the truth that the amount of money borrowed is not ours and we must respect the right of the owner in every circumstance.

Many times I have seen situations similar to the following: A man, whom we will call Peter, borrows money from a friend, whom we will call Bob, assuring him that he will pay him at a certain predetermined date. Nevertheless, when the time agreed upon to repay the money comes, Peter does not pay Bob. In most cases, Bob continues to wait patiently and is embarrassed to ask for his money. During this time, Peter does not feel obligated to repay the money. He reasons that Bob has plenty of money and does not need the money he borrowed. Peter believes that his own need for the money justifies the act of not respecting the due date for repaying the money.

Finally, Bob's patience begins to run out and he dares to ask for his money. Peter responds with an excuse and a false promise. Worse, Peter does not feel grateful to Bob for his help, but instead becomes angry because he believes Bob does not need the money. He then judges Bob as inconsiderate and selfish. Peter avoids any contact with Bob in order to escape the obligation he has to pay him, and their friendship may be ruined.

To God, Peter's reasoning is corrupt, and his act of keeping Bob's money is a form of robbery. If we rob someone and are picked up by the police, would they let us go simply because we express our intention of giving the money back later? Of course not. Our intentions do not alter justice and the law. In the same way, when the time comes to repay borrowed money, and we do not do it and justify our actions with false reasoning, our reasoning does not alter the just law that God has given. God says that such practice is sin, and the one who commits this sin is wicked.

In some cases, the owner does not threaten to take other measures or demand that the agreement be kept, because he is a kind and patient person or because the owner happens to be a benevolent institution. It is not ethical to take advantage of this kindness. Instead, we should show the owner of the money that we are conscious of the owner's right and are grateful for his patience.

We can do this through direct, continual, and respectful communication regarding our intentions and the circumstances related to the debt. We can also show the owner respect and gratefulness by being willing to make some kind of payment. There is a great difference between doing something and doing nothing. If the owner is willing to make the sacrifice of waiting patiently, even though he has the right to demand the money, we should show that we are also making a sacrifice by limiting needs and avoiding expenses in order to pay a part of the debt. In this way, we demonstrate an attitude of respect for what is ethical.

This was the case in the story of Karla and Alexander in the preface (see page IX). If Karla had humbled herself before God and thought about what was correct and ethical, she would have made the effort to show gratefulness to Alexander for his kindness to her. She could have done this by being thrifty for a while in order to give back to Alexander what belonged to him. If she was not able to pay on time, she could have asked for forgiveness and continued to be in communication with him, respectfully letting him know of her progress and plan for paying back the money. With this responsible and respectful attitude, God would have helped her get out of debt and regain a good reputation. In this case, it could have even resulted in a strong recommendation for a good job.

Of course, if we are the lender, we are also responsible to consider what is ethical regarding our attitude and actions. Although we have the right to do what we want as the lender, we should understand that everything belongs to the One who created all things – God. God requires that what is his be used in a way that reflects his character and will. God gives us the right to what he has placed in our power, but he doesn't give us the right to be antagonistic or cruel, or to disregard a poor person's dilemma.

Much depends on the attitude that a lender observes in the borrower. If the borrower responds deceitfully and uses the money for other expenses or vices, the lender should not show patience and consideration. He would be rewarding wrongdoing and encouraging those wrong actions. On the other hand, if the borrower shows respect and tries to be responsible and faithful but is hindered by circumstances of poverty, trials, or tragedies, the lender should try to show the compassion, patience, and help that God shows to the righteous in those circumstances.

This could involve postponing payments or reducing the amount of each payment while extending the deadline for the debt to be repaid. Also, the lender could consider forgiving the debt as in Matthew 18:23-35, which, although not teaching specifically about financial debt, uses the example of debt to show how we must be compassionate. As always, the important thing is to consider and practice what is ethical.

An important point to remember is that God specifically prohibits suing a fellow church member before authorities of this world. God says it is shameful that those who have been regenerated, who have the Holy Spirit for discernment and guidance, and who have been given the promise and future responsibility of reigning and judging the world and the angels should have to resort to the judgment of unbelievers to solve their problems. In 1 Corinthians 6:1-7, God exhorts us to suffer loss and allow ourselves to be defrauded before bringing this kind of shame to his name and to the church.

What To Do With Lost Possessions

Finally, we should consider that there are also principles of ethics dealing with possessions that others have lost which we have found. We have discussed God's command in the law of Moses that says if a person finds an animal, garment, or other possession that someone has lost, he is responsible to return the possession to the owner. This responsibility includes taking care of the lost possession in his own home until the owner claims it.

This law illustrates how God has made us responsible to care for the possessions of others. In general, society has abandoned what is ethical in this area. The attitude toward others' possessions has degenerated so much that many people automatically consider something lost forever if they forgot it or left it somewhere.

In past times, practicing what is ethical was the only acceptable behavior, but now that seems to be only a dream. Years ago my relatives not only left their homes unlocked when they left town, but left a note on the door announcing their absence and inviting people in to make themselves at home. They also told them what they could find in the refrigerator. They had complete trust that others would take care of their home and only take what they had permission to take.

What a contrast this is to our times when homes are locked and protected by tall fences and iron bars. Even then, homeowners do not feel completely comfortable when they leave. How much has been lost because what is ethical is not practiced and taught to our children!

Some years ago, *Reader's Digest* conducted an honesty test in a number of cities around the world. They left ten wallets with money and the owner's identification to see how many people would return them. Although one city had a large percentage of wallets returned, the great majority experienced the opposite. In Mexico, the percentage of wallets returned was zero. Some would laugh about this statistic because they know the situation so well, but no one laughs when they live the misery of being affected by this lack of ethics.

Some have the attitude that if so many other people abandon all ethics regarding lost items, they are also justified in doing so. Others have the dignity of not wanting to harm their reputation. They appreciate the value of doing what is ethical. They don't believe that the act of finding something automatically makes them the owner of it. They respect the right of owners and make themselves responsible to restore lost items to their rightful owners.

People who practice what is ethical have an attitude of serving and helping. They take action when something is in a position to be stolen, letting the owner know, and caring for the possessions of others. Reestablishing this practice of caring for others' property is a worthy cause for which to contend. We can do this by setting the example, teaching these principles to the children in our homes, requiring this kind of example and teaching in our schools, exalting good examples of ethical practice, and denouncing practices of what is not ethical.

The Golden Rule given by Jesus states, *Therefore all things whatsoever ye would that men should do to you, do ye even so to them.*[32] If we find something that is lost, this Golden Rule is the answer to what should be done. If we practice what is ethical in this manner, we are people of great esteem on this earth.

If in the past we fell to the temptation of keeping what belonged to another, we can always reject that path of life and determine to take the path of what is ethical from this point on. No matter how difficult it may seem, great satisfaction comes in asking for forgiveness and restoring or paying for what was taken. Far from resulting in shame, this precious humility will result in honor.

Of course, the amount of time and effort invested is limited before determining there is no reasonable hope of finding the owner of a lost item. As long as the law does not prohibit it, what has been found can then be treated as one's own possession if no one claims it. The line, however, is not very clear in this situation, making it better to lean toward waiting longer than not waiting long enough.

Worse than keeping what someone lost is keeping an item that belongs to someone else simply because it is possible to do so. This often happens in hotels. Hotel owners allow their clients to use and keep consumable items such as toilet paper, tissues, soap, and shampoo. But by no means do they consider towels, sheets, pillows, and other nondisposable articles to be in this category. Taking these items is an act of thievery and the furthest thing from the practice of what is ethical. Restaurants, libraries, offices, and other businesses suffer loss in the same manner. Once again, the Golden Rule is the answer.

---

32   Matthew 7:12.

Chapter 4

Ethical Handling of Finances

The apostle Paul warned Timothy that the root of all evil is the love of money. Much of the persecution Paul experienced with the Gentiles involved money and religion. He witnessed how great the power of money is over a man. Unfortunately, this power has resulted in many violations of what is ethical in the administration, use, and management of finances. The violations in this area have destroyed friendships, marriages, churches, and careers. They have affected entire societies. Considering the potential destructiveness of circumstances related to finances, we should pay special attention to the principles of ethics that will protect us from this damage.

Personal Finances

Let us first consider our own finances. Just saying "our own finances" reveals what is the root of the problem. When we think that the money and possessions we have are ours alone, we are forgetting that God the Creator is the legitimate owner of everything that exists. The well-being of our relationships depends upon practicing what is ethical, which is based upon the divine laws and attitudes of God. Clearly then, forgetting God's right in the area of finances causes many problems. Good ethics in relation to our own finances is based upon a humble recognition that *The earth is the LORD's, and the fulness thereof; the world, and they that dwell therein.*[33]

God is interested in the issue of finances. First, it has the

---
[33] Psalm 24:1.

potential to bring honor or dishonor to his name. Second, God loves all men and desires to guide them in finances to protect them from damage and secure their well-being. Third, he has plans and purposes for man and for the world that are of greater importance than simple financial stability. At times, he uses financial situations to bring about certain conditions to fulfill these purposes.

God has established principles about handling our finances, or rather the finances he has put in our hands. These principles are divided into two classes – obtaining money and using money. When we speak about obtaining money, we find many methods that are obviously evil, such as stealing or falsifying checks. On the other hand, some ways of obtaining money are good and acceptable, such as work or inheritance.

Work has been a part of God's plan for mankind since the beginning of history, when he put man in charge of the land that he created. Work became more difficult when the earth was cursed because of man's sin, but the responsibility to work never changed. God gave intelligence and talent to man. He gave him value as an important individual in his universal plan. Man has the capability of being creative, efficient, and productive in his work and of making his burden easier. God is pleased to see man take the initiative to prosper and develop the capabilities he gave him. Also, God promises to help man prosper if he will show faith and appreciate the superiority of God's wisdom, purposes, and ways.

Some ways of obtaining money are not obviously good or evil. In these cases, we must consider what is ethical in each situation to discern what is correct or incorrect. Doubtful ways of obtaining money relate to the type of work and purpose of the work.

We must consider two kinds of work. The first involves objects or services. This includes the production of necessary and discretionary items, the sale of these items, and their maintenance or repair. This can include medical services or anything that involves the body's physical condition. In this type of work, an ethical problem may affect people's spiritual or moral lives.

In the great majority of work involving objects or services, there is no moral or spiritual implication. For example, farming or raising animals to provide food fulfills a need or delight without any moral implication. However, those who sow, reap, or sell plants that are used for illegal drugs, smoking, or alcoholic beverages are participating in something that has destroyed lives and families. These cases create clear conflicts with the principles of what is ethical.

What complicates this is the fact that there are many jobs related to the production and provision of these harmful objects. These jobs vary from a direct relationship to an indirect relationship. For example, a technician or mechanic who works for someone who produces something illegal is involved in the work in an indirect way. A technician or mechanic who has his own shop where he sells and repairs devices or machinery is less involved, but still has a significant degree of involvement. Those who work cleaning and maintaining the repair shops are much less involved. Those who manufacture or sell common parts, like spark plugs or screws that are used for an illegal activity, are not involved, in spite of the evil use of their products.

Much work is indirectly involved in the production or provision of articles that are morally or physically harmful. However, knowing and applying the principles of ethics helps in making correct decisions before God and society about participating in a certain job.

Doing what is ethical protects us from that uncomfortable feeling of guilt that results from a false moral system. This is the other extreme. Some people promote ideas and philosophies that are different or even contrary to what God teaches. They establish a new moral level based upon their own criteria. The principles of what is ethical reveal how false those criteria are and how far they are from the divine laws of God.

One of these false moral systems proclaims the "evil" of killing animals for meat or using their hides for clothing. No one who practices what is ethical doubts that it is disgraceful to torture an animal for the sadistic delight of seeing them suffer. However, some people attempt to change the true meaning of what is cruelty. They define the common practice of killing animals for food as God commanded, and has been the custom throughout the ages, as cruelty. These deceivers attempt to raise their own criteria above that of God and force it upon the consciences and lives of those who are ignorant of the true principles of what is ethical.

Another example is when some people consider plants and trees to be of equal value to human beings and declare that it is "immoral" to use these for our benefit. Even replenishing what is used and preventing damage to the environment makes no difference to them. One final example of false morality is likening the use of weapons for defense or sport with the criminal use of weapons.

The second kind of work to consider relates to objects or services that help with spiritual, intellectual, or emotional needs. The relationship of this work to the subject of what is ethical is important because its purpose involves influence. The damage that material objects can cause to people's lives is great, but it cannot compare to the damage to people's lives and to entire societies that is caused by the power of incorrect influence. On the other hand, correct influence is the greatest and most important benefit that a person or society can experience. This type of work forms ideas and character, and teaches, transmits, and publishes ideas and information. Teachers, ministers, psychologists, politicians, writers, and mass media workers are examples of influential workers.

When the influence of ideas or information is good according to the principles of what is ethical, the workers in these jobs are not only earning a living; they are also sowing a good influence in the minds of people. However, if the influence of ideas or information is ungodly, those workers are committing a serious violation of what is ethical. Many jobs are directly or indirectly related to the production and provision of harmful ideas or information and, depending on the relationship, may or may not be contrary to what is ethical.

Sometimes we should abandon an unethical job as quickly as possible. When there is doubt, we must apply the four principles of what is ethical to the situation and sincerely analyze whether or not we can continue in this line of work. With sincere and humble analysis, we must ask ourselves questions in order to have a clear understanding of the situation. Would the apostles of Jesus have dedicated themselves to that job? Is working in that job a good example for children and for other Christians?

Author T. B. Maston in his book *Bueno o Malo? (Right or Wrong)*[34] suggests three tests to determine if something is correct. The first is the test of secrecy. This test is the answer to the question: *Do you not want someone to know about this?* The second is the test of totality, which is the answer to the question: *Should everyone in the world do this?* The third is the test of prayer, which asks, *Can I pray about this?*

Pablo Alberto Deiros also deals with the subject of analyzing situations in relation to what is ethical. In his book, *El Cristiano y los Problemas Éticos (The Christian and Ethical Problems)*, he suggests six questions that help determine what is ethical in any given situation:

---

34 T. B. Maston, *Bueno o Malo? (Right or Wrong?)*, ed. W. M. Pinson, Jr. 1990 (El Paso. Casa Bautista de Publicaciones, 1957).

On our part, besides what has been said, we can establish at least six limiting questions about a certain subject. First, does it bring glory to God? (1 Corinthians 10:31) Second, is this helpful? Or in other words, will this help my Christian life, testimony, and service? (1 Corinthians 10:23) Third, does it edify my Christian character and will it help me edify my brothers in the faith? (2 Corinthians 10:8) Fourth, will it lead me to slavery, bondage, and vice? (1 Corinthians 6:12) Fifth, will it strengthen me against temptation? (1 Timothy 6:11) And sixth, is this of the world or of the father? (1 John 2:16)[35]

These questions will help us have a clear understanding about whether a job is ethical or not. Of course, these questions can and should be applied to all issues that we deal with.

Besides work, many other ways of obtaining money that are not obviously good or bad must also be considered. Today we are often offered ways to make money that seem to eliminate the need for work, creativity, and initiative. Some of these are simply innocent prizes, but others require investments that can affect the economic well-being of our lives and that of others.

The pyramid scheme is an example of this. One person gives a sum of money to another who is higher up in the pyramid and has the right to receive perhaps ten times that sum from people lower on the pyramid. With limited discernment, we might only think about receiving ten times our investment without working. We might fail to notice that even if this scheme functions perfectly, the people at the very bottom of the pyramid will not receive anything from anyone. For them, it will result in being plundered. So many people have been hurt by this scheme that the government has had to make it illegal.

However, apart from the legality of such schemes, the principles of what is ethical reveal how incorrect they are. God

---

[35] Pablo Alberto Deiros, *El Cristiano y los Problemas Éticos* (*The Christian and Ethical Problems*) (El Paso: Casa Bautists de Publicaciones, 1977).

expresses his dislike toward these schemes, saying, *He that hasteth to be rich hath an evil eye, and considereth not that poverty shall come upon him.*[36] Knowing about his dislike for such things and the harm that others will suffer, is there humility before God and others if we become involved in a pyramid? Does it show responsibility, respect toward others, and protection of what is important to God? Of course it does not.

Other ways of obtaining money are not illegal because the harm caused is not so clear. Unfortunately, the governing officials themselves benefit. Lotteries, casinos, and raffles are examples. What is wrong with these? Don't we have the right to risk a little money with the hope of being a winner of much more? If we are going to waste money on soda pop and sweets, is it worse to risk it in a casino game? Are not lotteries for the public benefit in the end? Many justify participation in such things by asking questions like this.

These activities appear to be different from the pyramid scheme because in a pyramid there is the expectation to win. In casino games, lotteries, or raffles there is a clear possibility of losing as well as winning. We take the risk with an understanding of those possibilities.

However, when we apply our principles of what is ethical to these moneymaking schemes, we encounter problems. First, they go against what God said about greed being the motivation of *[he] that hasteth to be rich*. We might say, "That is not my problem. I am content with what I have, and I am only playing for the fun of seeing if I win, as in any game, sport, or competition." It may very well be that greed is honestly not the problem. But we know very well that for others it is. What is ethical always requires consideration for the well-being of others. "But they know what they are doing, and they don't have to do it," we might say. This is the most common conclusion

---

36 Proverbs 28:22.

and is very wrong. Here we find the subtle difference between the harm that comes from pyramids and the harm that comes from gambling. People in pyramids are harmed by the nature of the pyramid; people who gamble are harmed by the nature of people.

Physical forces control the mind and will of a person addicted to alcohol or drugs. In the same way, a psychological force controls the mind and will of people addicted to the hope of winning at gambling. The temptation that an alcoholic or drug addict experiences when he is offered alcohol or drugs is no different from the temptation that a gambling addict experiences when he is offered the opportunity to play the games.

It is difficult for someone not addicted to alcohol or drugs to understand the force of this addiction. Likewise, it is difficult for someone not addicted to gambling to understand the force of this addiction. However, the evidence in our society demonstrates this power and makes us responsible not to harm others or take advantage of their weaknesses. What they are doing is sin and they are responsible to God for their actions, but tempting them instead of protecting and rescuing them is no less sinful. Gambling has enslaved multitudes, resulting in families' source of income being plundered, homes being destroyed, and children being destined to poverty. These gambling addicts often resort to crime in the same way drug addicts do, in order to satisfy their desire or pay their debts.

Knowing this, is there any doubt that these practices are not ethical? God's way to obtain money is secure in producing prosperity and well-being for man. There is no substitute for honest work, creativity, initiative, saving, and wise administration of money for the well-being of an individual and of society.

Having considered the principles related to obtaining money, we must also consider the principles of what is ethical in the matter of spending money. As always, some things we spend money on are bad without any doubt, such as paying for objects or services that are vices or sin. We do not need to discuss the evil of such use of money.

The wrong in other types of spending is not so clear, however, because the error is not an issue of paying for something evil, but rather the lack of maintaining correct priorities. For example, buying a new car is not wrong in itself. However, if the car payments result in not being able to provide for the needs and well-being of the family, then buying the car could be a serious violation of what is ethical. Spending money on sports, trips, decorations, investments, or luxury can be either good or bad in the same way. God's Word says, *But if any provide not for his own, and specially for those of his own house, he hath denied the faith, and is worse than an infidel.*[37] We see that what is ethical not only relates to spending money for correct things, but also with correct priorities.

Other principles of concern in spending are those of balance and moderation. In other words, we should avoid overindulgence in any area of life; we should maintain integrity and respect for God; and we should be a good example for the family and other people.

The story of Ananias and Sapphira is a classic example of how people can use money in a way that appears to be correct, but in reality is corrupt. Acts chapter 5 tells how Ananias and Sapphira wanted to give something to the church just as others had been doing. They sold some property to obtain money to give but decided to give only a part of the money. Apparently, they were either vain and materialistic or they felt guilty and embarrassed for their lack of faith and did not want the others to know this. They brought their offering as if it were the full price of the property. They did not consider what was ethical in relation to that decision.

---

37 1 Timothy 5:8.

In this case, being ethical would have saved their lives. If they had been humble before God and man, practicing responsibility, respect, and protection of the desires of God, they would not have fallen to the temptation to lie to God. At the time, the church was just beginning to expand. Because their example would have grave consequences to other churches in the future, God chose to put a stop to the temptation to lie by showing his displeasure by taking their lives.

Their error was not giving only a part of the price of the property. They were giving a special offering voluntarily out of love and faith, and they had the liberty to give what they wanted according to their free will. The error was in being dishonest with God himself because they were dealing with the church. We see that what is ethical in our financial dealings with the church is of great importance to God and must be done honestly.

Many years ago, a man in our church committed a similar error. He promised to give a certain amount of tithes and another amount of offerings for the construction of the church buildings. However, he worked for the church, and the tithe of his salary was a known amount. His dishonesty in promising half of his tithe and the other half as an offering was obvious. What we must learn is that God is not so much interested in the amount given as he is in the integrity with which it is given. If an offering does not show integrity, instead of being a blessing, it is rebellion.

During the ministry of Christ, the Pharisees had an unethical custom related to their offerings. They would go to public places where many people could see them give to charity. They would even blow trumpets to attract the attention of the public when giving. Jesus said they did this because they desired the glory and praise of man. However, according to Jesus, this vain desire for the glory of man was displeasing to God. He said that the only reward for their offering was the praise that they sought. He also taught us that our Father in heaven will give a true reward to those who give without seeking glory for themselves.

We must clarify the fact that giving in secret does not so much refer to the visibility of the offering as it does to the issue of seeking the glory. This becomes clear when we consider that Barnabas humbly brought the price of his property before the feet of the apostles, and it was very pleasing to God. The poor widow put two small coins in the offering at the temple in front of Christ, not to be seen, but rather because that was the place where the offerings were given. What displeases God is the desire to get attention for ourselves to win the praise of man.

There are some church members who do not participate with the rest of the congregation in giving their regular tithes and offerings. However, when there is a special project that is very visible, they are delighted to publicly declare the amount of their offering. Such vanity is far from being ethical.

Sometimes people feel the desire and right to maintain control over the use of their offerings. Church members who give their regular tithes and offerings understand that the offerings belong to God, and their use will be determined by the church and whoever is authorized for that purpose. Unfortunately, some members think the money they give is still theirs when it comes to deciding how it will be used. The error in this consists primarily in making their money appear to be tithes and offerings, when in reality their desire to maintain control makes it a specially designated offering. Since they do not actually give tithes and offerings, they are disobedient to the teachings of God. Giving money as if it were regular tithes and offerings when it is not is dishonest. Then, those who have greater income and give a greater amount look down on others who give smaller amounts, even though the percentage given is the same. This also is an act of vanity.

Of course, we could honestly express our willingness to contribute to a certain project apart from our regular offerings. Then it is a matter of an agreement, and if we both respect the agreement, there is no lack of ethics. An important point to clarify here is that this offering is given in addition to regular biblical offerings.

A man that I knew offered one of our churches a piece of property in a pretty location in the mountains where he suggested that we build a camp or retreat. However, this was under the condition that he maintain control of the property. He was not a member of the church and did not faithfully attend the services. He did not give tithes and offerings and did not trust that the church could undertake this ministry by itself. Because of this, I knew that the mutual trust and principles of ethics required to maintain a common purpose for the future was lacking, and it would not have been wise to proceed.

In other cases, mutual trust and a correct example do exist, which establish the foundation for an agreement that will benefit all. What is ethical is always the basis of correct and wise decisions.

Finances in a Marriage

In no relationship is it more important to practice financial ethics than in a marriage. Finances have the potential to bring much blessing to a marriage, but they also have the potential to cause much conflict. In a study conducted by the Consumer Credit Counseling Service (CCCS) of people who came to the organization for debt or budget counseling, 60 percent of the married respondents reported fighting about money with their spouses. More than 93 percent reported that financial problems increased the amount of stress in their lives (CCCS 2003).[38]

---

38 Carolyn Washburn and Darlene Christensen, "Financial Harmony: A key component of successful marriage relationship," *http://ncsu.edu/ffci/publications/2008/v13-n1-2008-spring/Washburn-Christensen.php* (Spring 2008).

ETHICAL HANDLING OF FINANCES

Many couples have asked me if they should handle the finances in a marriage together or separately. The two main reasons for this question are fear of conflict and desire to maintain control for their own security. These concerns may be important but are not a part of God's plan for marriage.

What is the answer to this question if we apply the principles of what is ethical? We know God has said that in marriage there are no longer two individuals, but the two are made one. This implies harmony in spirit, purpose, and destiny, all of which satisfy deep needs and lead to a life of mutual love and joy. Experiencing this ideal relationship depends on the degree of consecration of each spouse to God, trusting fully in the superiority of his intelligence in his plan for marriage. A godly couple will earnestly desire to conform to his commands with a confident security that he will lead them to the very best relationship.

This relationship requires a great degree of giving ourselves to the other, of acceptance, and of unconditional love. As a result, it will be natural to handle finances together. Handling them separately becomes a barrier to harmony because the motivation to do so is fear of errors, distrust, or selfishness. We might feel more secure, but the goal of having one of the most precious experiences in life would be sacrificed.

This ideal situation does not work automatically. We must know and practice what is ethical. Far from being an unreachable goal, it is the normal situation that God has established. To understand how this works, we must understand four different "levels of motivation" and experience.[39]

The most visible level consists of what we do and what we say. Why do we do and say those things? This question leads us to the second level that consists of our attitudes or ways of

---

39 My explanation of these four levels is a variation on the "Four Levels of Conflict" taught by Bill Gothard in the Institute in Basic Life Principles.

thinking. Where do these ways of thinking come from? The answer, and the third level, is that they are conclusions that have been formed based on our values or what we feel is of the greatest importance. The fourth level reveals the source of our values, which is either God's power and wisdom or our own will and power.

Although these four levels apply to all human experience, let us consider them in relation to finances in marriage. If we trust that the wisdom of God is superior and desirable, and that only through his power will there be security, we will form values that come from God. Material things will not be comparable in value to integrity and harmony in marriage. Our security will not compare in value to the good reputation of taking care of our partner. Opportunities to earn money will not be equal in value to faith in God's provision and blessing.

These values, in turn, will form the couple's way of thinking. We will be thinking about how to care for the well-being of our spouse instead of ourselves. The husband will understand his obligation, as head of the marriage, to be wise, prudent, and responsible in the financial decisions he makes in order to care for his wife and family. The wife will understand her obligation, as her husband's suitable helper, to be respectful, to help him practice discipline in financial matters, to help with wise counsel, and to honor him with trust, patience, and contented submission. We will strive to be responsible, prudent, and frugal to achieve fulfillment in the mutual protection of the marriage. These ways of thinking will produce behavior and a lifestyle where everything is managed together with responsibility, humility, and love for each other.

If the husband fails in something, the wife will have patience. She might need to respectfully help chart a wiser course for the future. She will also recognize and demonstrate that the most important thing in financial matters is to maintain a relationship that is healthy and pleasing to God. The husband will also recognize this and will not only learn to improve the situation, but will also demonstrate his capacity to recognize and change the error. This will result in greater trust. What a precious ideal and what a desirable life can be experienced when we follow God faithfully and practice what is ethical.

Sadly, many do not experience this because they do not believe and accept the superiority of God's wisdom. Being led by the will of God does not seem as good as their way. Their values, ways of thinking, and behavior will demonstrate this lack of trust in God. If we seek our own way in marriage instead of the will of God, the matter of what is ethical will not be essential.

The matter of ethics is of great importance also when one spouse sincerely desires to be submitted to God's will, but the other does not. What is the ethical thing to do when a person is married to someone who is not trustworthy in handling finances? Sometimes this is simply the result of laziness or carelessness. Other times people deceive, abuse, and take advantage of their own spouse in money matters.

The temptation is for a spouse to abandon what is ethical and defend himself or herself by accusing, rebuking, threatening, having secret practices, or even by ending the marriage through separation or divorce. There is no doubt about the lack of what is ethical in these responses. The other extreme is for the spouse to suffer abuse throughout life because he or she believes this is the only option for one who is submitted to God. The error of this extreme is not clear and requires consideration and application of the principles of what is ethical to respond properly.

We know that what is ethical requires humility before God and before others. Because of this, we must exhibit patience with another's weaknesses and the capability to forgive errors with the purpose of strengthening character and edifying the other over a period of time. However, even God, in spite of his great patience and mercy, has limits. When patience and love are belittled and used as an opportunity to take advantage of another, those virtues lose their beneficial effect, and instead of helping, they can contribute to the formation of corrupt habits. When someone gets to this point, God gives steps to correct the errors instead of continuing with patient exhortation. Additionally, in some cases, Christ said that humble and noble responses are useless and inappropriate. He exhorted us to *Give not that which is holy unto the dogs, neither cast ye your pearls before swine, lest they trample them under their feet, and turn again and rend you.*[40]

What we learn is that there must be a correct balance between patience and firmness. In financial situations, we must be able to forgive faults and have patience in order to wait for God's work of edification in the life of another. However, when the abuse becomes a conscious and continuous way of life, there is no obligation to suffer abuse without taking steps to correct the situation. In this case, we must be careful not to fall into the errors of bitterness, spite, or vengeance. However, we must be firm in demonstrating to a spouse that he or she is being abusive, and even though we will continue to love and serve the other, we will not be an accomplice in the development and practice of bad habits.

In some cases, this implies not preventing consequences that result from dishonest or irresponsible practices. Many wives think they are doing right when they continually pay whatever price is necessary so their husband will not suffer consequences for his wrong behavior. In reality, if this is a continual practice, they are not doing the right thing, but rather are eliminating precisely what the husband needs in order to learn responsibility.

If we touch a hot stove and are burned, the pain is very

---

40 Matthew 7:6.

displeasing but necessary to teach us to be more careful with our hands. If we do not feel pain, we might keep the hand on the stove until it is seriously damaged. In the same way, we need to experience difficult and displeasing consequences when we do wrong in order to learn not to live that way. Losing possessions, work, or even freedom is the only thing that can rescue some people. Suffering these temporary consequences can be of great benefit over time.

In other cases, the separate management of possessions and income is necessary. This is not the ideal situation. However, in cases of continuous abuse, it may be necessary. Without bitterness or lack of compassion, a spouse must express his or her spiritual reasons for considering this type of separation, the necessary conditions for it, and his or her desire to return to mutual harmony and management if there is a proven, sincere change in the attitudes of the abuser. Maintaining this goal of returning to what is ideal is important. The spouse must not become so accustomed to another way of life that when it becomes possible to achieve the ideal, the spouse will refuse because he or she is rooted in a different way of living.

Finances That Belong to Others
Problems can also arise in the handling of money that belongs to others. Many circumstances exist in which we manage money or possessions that belong to another person or organization. As always, it is not necessary to mention practices that are directly condemned by God, such as when an usher steals money from the offerings or other instances of deceit, dishonesty, and fraud. What we must consider are the practices that are not clearly seen as wrong but which cause conflicts that damage reputations. Practicing what is ethical will help us to avoid going through these situations and suffering the damage they cause.

We might have the opportunity to manage the finances

of another as part of our profession or as a voluntary service. Whichever the case, what is ethical consists of, most importantly, a clear and firm attitude that the decisions made in the management of another person's finances must represent the will and well-being of that person and not our own. If the money does not belong to us, its management is not for our personal benefit. This may seem clear for many people, but the number of people who fall into the temptation to obtain personal benefit from another's finances is amazing.

Many years ago, a church had invited a preacher for a series of special meetings. After one meeting, a pastor invited the preacher, together with many members of that pastor's family, relatives, and leaders of the church, including me, to one of the most expensive restaurants in town. When it became clear to me that this pastor intended to pay the account of all of his guests with money from the church, I was embarrassed and ashamed. The church had not agreed to pay for so many people in a luxurious restaurant and did not even know about it. The majority of the members had low incomes and would never take their own families to that place. Furthermore, all of the invited guests could easily have paid their own bill.

This is an example of someone obtaining a personal benefit from money that was under his care but that did not belong to him. He exhibited no humility before God or the church to seek the agreement of the other members or to limit himself to circumstances that the rest of the church may have been able to afford. Instead of responsibility toward the church, respect for its will, and protection of God's interests, he had an attitude of power and liberty to fulfill his own desire and seek personal benefit.

Of course, if a church or other organization agrees about this kind of expenditure, then there is nothing wrong with

ETHICAL HANDLING OF FINANCES

spending the money, as long as a person demonstrates what is ethical with humility and moderation.

Another pastor, a good man, lost his ministry because he fell to the temptation to buy excessive amounts of gasoline for personal trips with the church's money. Nothing causes more distrust, suspicion, and bad feelings than the mismanagement of money that belongs to others. Because of this, we must establish clear and careful practices in order to avoid such distrust and suspicion.

Transparency in the management of another person's money is very important. We should not have to hide anything. Those to whom the money legitimately belongs should be able, at all times, to see that it is being handled with honesty and responsibility. A few recommendations or bits of counsel about this kind of careful transparency are as follows: We should make sure that another trusted person is present when we count someone else's money. This is necessary so there will be a witness to our honesty. In the handling of an organization's checkbook, we should require more than one signature on a check, even if the organization insists that they trust us in handling the checkbook. Detailed records of all income and expenses are indispensable. Trust is something precious, but it can be lost over a matter of cents.

Financial reports should be available to all of those who have a right to the information, and should be offered voluntarily to demonstrate the care that we are practicing. Agreements about expenditures should be clear so that major expenses are decided by the organization or its representatives, while minor expenditures may be authorized by trusted personnel. When we are trusted with making a certain amount of expenditures, we should be careful with that trust and avoid any appearance of personal gain. If there is doubt about whether an expense is major or minor, we should always make the safest decision and show how much we care about doing what is ethical.

Up to this point, we have seen how practicing what is ethical can prevent damage to relationships, reputations, functional organization, financial well-being of families, and many other situations. A great number of problems can be avoided or eliminated. The beauty of what is ethical, however, is that it is not only useful to prevent damage, but also to enhance the quality of good in positive practices. What is ethical will not only get us out of a difficult situation; it will raise us to new heights of good.

Chapter 5

Hospitality – Why Our "Best" is Not Always Right

The practice of hospitality shows how the principles of what is ethical raise our dignity and culture. Paul mentions hospitality to the Romans[41] as a characteristic of a life dedicated to the Lord. When he gave Timothy instructions regarding the widows in the church, he named hospitality as one of the signs of virtue in those women.[42] In the book of Hebrews, God exhorts, *Be not forgetful to entertain strangers: for thereby some have entertained angels unawares.*[43] Hospitality is not something that is either practiced or not practiced. Instead, it is a light that can shine either dimly or brightly. There are levels of hospitality, and the practice of what is ethical takes us to new heights in these levels.

For example, some men and women are admirable in their practice of hospitality toward others. However, at the same time they are giving attention and care to others, they might be sacrificing the attention and care needed by their own families. These principles help to elevate a person to a higher level and maintain a wise balance regarding hospitality. This makes him capable of guiding the family to show hospitality to others while not sacrificing the family time or well-being.

It is unfortunate that the kindness of hospitality a man shows to visitors, friends, or relatives can cause tension in his

---

41 Romans 12:13.
42 1 Timothy 5:9-10.
43 Hebrews 13:2.

relationship with his wife or children. Wives also, with good intentions, make their husbands feel unattended or even dishonored, while they dedicate themselves to showing hospitality to others. When our hospitality is based on what is ethical, we produce an attentiveness and good feeling in others and in our own family.

In addition to increasing the well-being of relationships, good ethics also increases the quality of hospitality shown. Concern about traditions, however, may limit the quality of hospitality. The traditions of hospitality are beneficial when they are formed by trying to make another person comfortable. They can be useful in teaching children, young people, newlyweds, and others who have little experience in how to practice what is ethical.

The problem with traditions is their mutability. They may have started with the focus on the well-being and comfort of others, but once they are formed, the focus can change. Rather than making it work for the good of another, the focus becomes keeping the tradition. This subtle change results in hospitality that is routine in nature and reduces the personal touch that is so important to the quality of hospitality.

For example, in Mexico we give a plastic fork along with a plate of food when we serve people at a group event. The focus of the servers may be the convenience of the people being served or simply the keeping of the tradition. If the focus is on helping the people to eat with ease, we will give a fork that is suitable for the food they are serving. If we are serving cake, the simplest plastic fork will be sufficient. If the food is chicken, beef, or something of a similar consistency, we should notice that a small plastic fork will be useless and difficult to use. In this case, we should provide an adequate fork accompanied by a knife. However, if our focus is on keeping the tradition of giving a fork, we might give forks that are not appropriate without thinking about the problem we are causing and the lack of quality in our hospitality.

For large birthday parties in Mexico, a piece of cake is served on a plastic plate with a paper napkin. The articles needed are given, but the napkin is placed underneath the piece of cake. As it absorbs the humidity and is stained by cake or frosting, it is not useable to clean one's mouth and hands. The tradition of serving cake with a napkin has been kept, but in all practicality, there is as much hassle as if there was no napkin given. Hospitality would be shown by providing another napkin separately.

This difference between the quality of hospitality based on what is ethical and the quality of hospitality based only on traditions or customs is apparent in all related matters. What is ethical involves not only providing food and housing, but also thinking in advance about the experience and taking measures to make the situation as comfortable as possible according to our ability. We should not only provide a room and a bed to sleep on, but also think about the comfort of the bed and the atmosphere that the guest will experience. Will he be too cold or too hot? Will there be too much light or noise? Are there disagreeable odors? Has the area been thoroughly cleaned? Is there privacy? We should consider all these questions and more in order to achieve the best experience possible for our guest.

It is important to understand that showing hospitality does not depend on the elegance or formality of the experience, but rather on the feeling of comfort. An elegant supper could be very comfortable for some people. Others, however, might be fearful of harming something or of acting improperly, which could make the experience very uncomfortable. Therefore, we should be careful not to base our hospitality on our own preferences or personal habits, but we should think about how another person may feel. We should provide an atmosphere in which others sense kindness, without unnecessary pressure or restrictions.

When food is served, we should think of hygiene and the comfort of the atmosphere. We should consider the preferences of the person being served and not our own preferences. Even the portions served will indicate a desire to show kindness without imposing upon the guests a sense of obligation. We should also take into consideration the customs of those being served when providing silverware, napkins, towels, soap, sheets, blankets, and other similar objects.

Of course, the display of hospitality also depends on the financial ability of the host. If we do the best we can with all that we have in order to show hospitality, thinking of the comfort of the guest, we have accomplished what is ethical. The gratitude that a person feels for the attentive hospitality of someone with few assets is no less than the gratitude he feels for the hospitality of someone with many assets. The attentive hospitality is noble and admirable in all cases, and no one should feel embarrassed for lacking financial resources.

My sister Doyla remembers that when we were young and poor, Mom would have guests over on Sunday night and serve grilled cheese sandwiches and root beer floats. That was easy and cheap, but delightful and hospitable.

Some traditions, nevertheless, should be universal and unchangeable. Guests should be served first in all cases. Even more importantly, God should be placed before all, honored in what each person does, and thanked in prayer before eating every meal.

Chapter 6

Ethical Agreements

In the same way that the practice of what is ethical increases the quality of hospitality, it also increases the quality of communication. Communication is a determining factor in the success of functional organization, projects, production, and personal relationships. With communication that is complete, clear, appropriate, and timely, a person or a group will have the necessary information to carry out plans.

When communication is not complete, clear, appropriate, and timely, we open the door for ignorance regarding details. This can cause mistakes and misunderstandings. It can harm the success of tasks and result in a loss of quality, time, or reputation. The inconvenience of not being properly informed or being misinformed can hurt relationships in businesses, organizations, churches, and the home.

In many cases, our communication represents our "word of honor." When we make a verbal agreement with someone, that person is not basing his communication on a lawful contract or on any item that is pawned or given for surety. That person is trusting that we are honest people who respect and honor what is right and reject what is evil. He is trusting that we value actions that are correct and that we value being known by God and others as honorable people.

The value of our word represents the value of us as people. We don't keep our word simply for some sort of benefit or to avoid a certain risk; we keep our word out of a sense of self-respect.

We won't take value away from our lives by following another path. Even when others are not honorable and do not expect us to be, we should not change, because we value honor and do not want to live in a way that is less than honorable. We should not sacrifice our word of honor.

If we can give our word of honor, we are more trustworthy than a formal contract. Some dishonorable men know how to twist or get out of legal contracts, but an honorable person would not do that even if he had the opportunity. To an honorable person, his word is of more value than any temporal benefit.

This is not only manifested in large matters, but also in small, everyday promises and responsibilities. Christ said, *He that is faithful in that which is least is faithful also in much.*[44] To an honorable person, even keeping a simple appointment represents his value as a person. For this reason, if we have given our word of honor to be at a certain place at a certain time, we recognize the need to keep the appointment for the sake of our word. It is not a light thing to miss an appointment with someone. If we are aware of a reason we will not be able to keep the appointment, we must do everything possible to communicate with the other person and explain the situation. If, due to circumstances out of our control or out of real urgency, we are not able to communicate beforehand, we must communicate as soon as possible to apologize and explain why we missed the appointment. Whether or not we are people of honor can be seen in every kind of promise and in every form of communication.

When we appreciate and live according to the principles of what is ethical, we humbly put the good of the Lord and others first; we are responsible to keep appointments and take care of responsibilities; we respect the person and position of others; and therefore, we protect the interests and good of others.

---

44   Luke 16:10.

We also recognize that both good and bad can result from the quality of communication, and there is never too much communication of pertinent information.

This will motivate us, first of all, to communicate all information related to a certain matter. Second, we will make sure the information has been understood. Third, we will make sure this information is given in plenty of time to be considered and used. By no means will we imagine or suppose that another has received and understood all the necessary information. Instead, we will confirm that this information has been effectively received. We will also be motivated to look for information in order to avoid making suppositions and act according to the facts in order to fulfill our assigned responsibilities. The knowledge and practice of what is ethical increases the quality of communication and the good results that this communication brings.

Chapter 7

Proper Behavior Between the Opposite Sex

Since what is ethical relates to matters that have to do with the harmony and well-being of relationships, a discussion of the subject of proper behavior between persons of the opposite sex is necessary. The enormous attraction between the sexes and the potential for lives, homes, churches, and careers to be hurt makes this one of the most important subjects. This study in ethics is to help establish a foundation for making wise decisions in situations that are not clearly defined. The Bible clearly outlines some situations as wrong, and others it clearly outlines as right. Other situations are not as clearly defined when it comes to behavior between men and women. In these situations, the application of what is ethical helps us do what is best without causing harm or embarrassment to ourselves or others.

Maintaining proper communication between opposite sexes is demonstrated in the example of Jesus and his disciples and the women who followed and ministered to them. Their behavior and communication were held at the level of friendship, loyalty to the truth, and common purpose as servants of God. Even when this is the focus of a relationship, however, the danger of temptation and inordinate affection exists. How can we enjoy proper communication and fellowship between opposite sexes and at the same time avoid the dangers?

The fact is that attraction is not something that is initiated or eliminated by an act of the will. Although attraction in itself is not wrong, the expression of that attraction or the forming of a more intimate relationship can be completely wrong. We know some circumstances and actions lend themselves to producing attraction. The knowledge and practice of the principles of ethics help us discern these circumstances to avoid the kind of communication that changes the focus in a relationship.

God created man and woman with the natural instinct of attraction, so they could look for their spouse, marry, experience great joy in their relationship, and fulfill his command to *Be fruitful, and multiply, and replenish the earth*.[45] Because of this, there is a difference in the matter of attraction for single people and for married people.

For single people, responsibility requires the control of a legitimate attraction toward different persons in order to develop spiritual friendships, until they have met the one with whom God would have them share their lives. Sometimes this attraction is experienced with only one person. Other times it is experienced with more than one person, which requires certain limitations while waiting to find the person who will be their wife or husband, and other limitations when they have found that special person. These limitations are not rules. They are the fruit of attitudes and actions that stem from the fundamental principles of what is ethical.

First, these single people must show *humility* before God, submitting to his order and will, and considering his purposes and thoughts as superior to their own in all things. Also, they will show humility before the authorities that God has established to give direction and counsel, such as parents and pastors. Second, they will consider their *responsibility* to God, family, and church when interacting with the opposite sex and in regard to the attraction they experience. Their responsibility

---

45   Genesis 1:28.

will be to live with dignity as an example that others will see and be able to follow.

Third, they will make sure that any interaction with the opposite sex shows *respect* for God's reputation and honor, for their own family, and for the family of the person with whom they are interacting. Fourth, they will feel the need and be determined to *protect* the interests, the will, and the good name of God, of their family, and of the person of the opposite sex, keeping the feeling of attraction under the control of the Holy Spirit.

When people marry, it is the will of God that the mutual attraction results in a loving and intimate relationship that fills both husband and wife with joy, satisfaction, and gratitude. Song of Solomon describes the intensity of this precious interaction within marriage. This does not mean they will never feel attraction for others or that others will not feel attraction for them. It means that the purpose for the attraction has been fulfilled, and the attraction they may feel for others will be in subjection to God. They will maintain their relationships with others on a level of friendship that is appropriate and is based on integrity and honor, accepting that there is no other legitimate end for the attraction in these other cases.

Violating what is ethical in matters of attraction is especially dangerous due to the power of this particular instinct. It has great potential for harming important relationships, our own reputation and honor, and even the reputation of God himself. In order to avoid this danger and practice what is ethical, we need to better understand the roots or subtle steps that start a chain of circumstances that gradually weakens the conscience and increases the attraction.

Frequently, the first step down this path occurs when we are alone with a person of the opposite sex. At first, attraction may not exist and the situation might appear to be innocent and harmless. However, the familiarity from spending time alone together can be conducive to producing attraction, and being alone allows that attraction to develop. The next step in this sequence is communication that is more and more personal. Intentions may be completely healthy and even spiritual, and both individuals may be edifying one another without any intention of causing weakness. Even so, this forms a trust that becomes progressively more intimate and has the power to affect the emotions and strongest desires of a human being.

With this more intimate trust, the next step is the use of more intimate language. Although at this point people already desire to experience the gratification of intimate communication, they could have noble intentions without realizing how close they are to a relationship that is beyond what is ethical and legitimate. During the development of these steps toward a more intimate trust, the situation is further complicated by the gradual development of physical contact. At first, this physical contact is only casual and traditional in nature. However, little by little, physical contact has the ability to produce more and more familiarity. At a certain point, the contact goes beyond what is traditional and casual to what is on purpose and gratifying.

These steps, which seem harmless in the beginning, have resulted in the fall and harm of multitudes. The danger should be taken seriously, and we should dedicate ourselves fervently to what is ethical to avoid beginning this gradual sequence.

At this point, we need to recognize that for married people, it is even more dangerous when they permit a negative sequence in the relationship with their spouse. In this case, while they are forming this kind of trust and familiarity with another person, a distancing occurs in the relationship with their own spouse. This distancing produces communication that is less personal and intimacy that is simply routine. Physical contact becomes less personal and even fake. What is sad and hurtful is the fact that gratification experienced with another person is deceitful, and after harming or destroying a marriage, the person realizes that the whole thing was simply an illusion. In place of happiness, they reap the misery and pain of having lost their true love.

Final Words

The result of trusting in the superior wisdom and intelligence of God and practicing what is ethical is peace, tranquility, stability, dignity, and transparency. We do not have to fear what others might know about our lives, and we do not have to pretend that we are something we are not. With a relaxed contentment and satisfaction, we can live with confidence, serve with true security, and rejoice in the development of personal relationships in which there is trust, loyalty, and love.

For some, this subject of what is ethical seems more like a matter of simple common sense. In certain parts of the world and in certain times in history, parents raised their children in the fear of God and in the knowledge of his Word. Society recognized the authority and superiority of God, and what is ethical really was a matter of common sense.

Unfortunately, in our day, most people have not had the benefit of education and discipline that are focused on the Word of God and the character of Christ. Because of this, we live in an age in which "common sense" is no longer common. Even in the church, as Paul said, *For all seek their own, not the things which are Jesus Christ's.*[46] Peter exhorted, *For the time is come that judgment must begin at the house of God.*[47] Even so, in every age, God has given light for us to know the path that is sure and profitable. He has done this so that we can discern what is prudent, wise, and ethical in every circumstance.

---

46 Philippians 2:21.
47 1 Peter 4:17.

ETHICAL

Dear reader, God desires to bless you and use you as an example before the world of the precious fruit of practicing what is ethical.

About the Author

Dr. Morris graduated from Pacific Coast Baptist Bible College and Anchor Theological Seminary. He received his PhD in biblical studies from Louisiana Baptist University. Since 1978, he and his wife, Debbie, have served as missionaries in Chiapas, Mexico. He presently pastors the Baptist church he founded in Tuxtla Gutiérrez and oversees several other churches, missions, and a Christian school. Much of his time is dedicated to training Hispanic pastors, and counseling.

To learn more about Dr. Morris and his wife, to pray for them, or support them, please do so by using the links below.

Visit: www.dandebbiemorris.com
Visit: www.ibbh.org (their Mexico church website)

If you have benefited from this book, please place a review on Amazon.com or on the other site where you purchased it or tell others about it on Facebook.

Also Available by Dr. Morris

Understand and unlock your mind's natural ability to memorize long passages

Called to be a missionary as a teenager, I had a great desire to fulfill God's will, but had a great sense of inadequacy for such an extraordinary purpose. But God says he who meditates in His Word ... shall be like a tree planted by the rivers of water, that bringeth forth his fruit in his season; his leaf also shall not wither; and whatsoever he doeth shall prosper (Psalm 1:3). This verse was and still is a great source of encouragement.

Part of meditation is to memorize God's Word, so I began a systematic method of memorizing consecutive passages of scripture. Through the years I learned, both by study and by experience, how God made our memory function. Presently, I have 42 chapters memorized and, best of all, our missionary work has prospered beyond what I could have imagined.

This book describes what I learned about permanently memorizing scripture and will help you be one of the few who experiences the blessing of meditation in God's Word, and the hope that whatsoever he doeth shall prosper.

In this book you'll learn:
- Specific memorization techniques.
- How to memorize scripture, the Bible.
- How to retain what you memorize

Available in English from:
Print (Amazon): http://amzn.to/1zxdjLn
eBook (Amazon): http://amzn.to/1EATntZ
Print (Aneko Press): http://goo.gl/K5a4eE

Available in Spanish from:
www.dandebbiemorris.com

www.ingramcontent.com/pod-product-compliance
Lightning Source LLC
Chambersburg PA
CBHW052109070526
44584CB00017B/2404